GROWING GREAT GIRLS

GROWING GREAT GIRLS

Ian and Mary Grant

RANDOM HOUSE
NEW ZEALAND

For more information about our titles go to www.randomhouse.co.nz
A catalogue record for this book is available from the National Library of New Zealand

A RANDOM HOUSE BOOK
published by
Random House New Zealand
18 Poland Road, Glenfield, Auckland, New Zealand

Random House International
Random House
20 Vauxhall Bridge Road
London, SW1V 2SA
United Kingdom

Random House Australia Pty Ltd
Level 3, 100 Pacific Highway,
North Sydney 2060, Australia

Random House South Africa Pty Ltd
Isle of Houghton
Corner Boundary Road and Carse O'Gowrie
Houghton 2198, South Africa

Random House Publishers India Private Ltd
301 World Trade Tower, Hotel Intercontinental Grand Complex
Barakhamba Lane, New Delhi 110 001, India

First published 2008

© 2008 Ian and Mary Grant

The moral rights of the authors have been asserted

ISBN 978 1 86941 895 3

Random House New Zealand uses non chlorine-bleached papers from sustainably
managed plantation forests

Cover design: Bruce Pilbrow, Parents Inc.
Cover photograph: Emily Jones
Design and layout: Sharon Grace
Printed in Australia by Griffin

Contents

To all the women in our lives who have contributed to make us the people we are and who have blessed us with their wisdom and feminine insight. To our mothers, grandmothers and great-grandmothers who were once girls and who became women of character and resourcefulness, leaving us a heritage of fine example, humour and leadership.

And to our three small granddaughters, Ariella, Petra and Ruby, who have won our hearts, and whom we hope will blossom in the stream of womanhood inherited from their mothers and grandmothers.

Ian and Mary Grant

Introduction

Listening to a girl's story will help her retain her own voice

Since the publication of *Growing Great Boys* many parents have asked when we would be writing a similar book on girls. To be perfectly honest, although we conduct 'hot tips' seminars on the subject of raising girls, and regularly read books and papers on girls in order to keep up with current research, we have been slightly hesitant about the idea of a book on the subject. In addition to our two adult sons, and one very lovely adult daughter, we have six young grandsons who have been very much part of our lives for the last seven or eight years. We haven't personally experienced close relationships with little girls in recent years.

At the same time, we were gradually convinced that there might be a place for a book of this genre on girls, and when our children last year presented us with the gift of three little granddaughters we started to become really motivated about the project. However, it is more than just our little granddaughters that has motivated us.

It seems that more than ever before our culture is becoming aggressive towards girls. Parents feel they are fighting a strong tide of commercial interests and media pressure. A cursory search of the internet will convince you that this is no illusion. It quickly becomes apparent that while those who work with pre-teens, such as teachers and mentors, consider 'tweenagers' to be between 10 and 12 years of age, marketers who target this category of young people consider 'tweenagers' to include seven- to 12-year-olds. The proliferation of pornography and the 'slut' culture pervasive in clothing and music trends, along with an individualistic approach to much of life, all work against a girl's healthy passage into adulthood.

We have spent many hours over the last few years hearing about tragic cases of rebellious girls whose lives have gone way off track. Not all of these situations could have been avoided, but the pain felt by their distressed parents — who by this time have usually been in need of specialist counselling — is palpable. One of our aims is to help parents by providing simple ideas and put in place practices, early in their daughters' lives, that might lead to a reduction in these situations.

On the other hand, it is a pleasure to meet self-assured young women living life with verve and optimism — young adults who, with the continued support of loving parents, are able to stretch their wings knowing they have been given strong roots and are well-equipped with the skills and self-knowledge to build a meaningful life. It has been an honour to watch our own daughter grow into a dignified, graceful adult, and a privilege to be parents to two daughters-in-law who possess great character and resourcefulness. All these women are confident and assured in their leadership and careers, and are great mothers.

We have written this book in the hope that in some way we will contribute to you having the best chance possible to enjoy your daughter, and the pleasure of one day launching a self-reliant, sure and loving young woman into the world. We want you to know why a girl's unique nature needs strong attachments, and to learn practical ways to provide these. And we want you to know that you can give your daughter resilience by mentoring her in a way that will provide her with inner strength and outward grace.

Counsellors have told us that, judging by OECD standards, here in New Zealand we have the equivalent of an epidemic of anorexia and bulimia among our young girls. The rate of abuse suffered by girls (the most recent studies say one in four girls is abused) and the pervasiveness of adolescent depression means we must fight for our girls and offer them the loving shelter and protection of our wisdom.

In contrast to these negative trends, this is also a time when there are more opportunities than ever before for girls to succeed. We need to provide for them a healthy and clear path through to adulthood, so they can take advantage of these opportunities. In rushing to treat boys and girls as equal could it be that we have neglected to honour something unique about girls, something that women have always recognised — the special and different nature of girls?

This book is mainly concerned with ways to make life with your daughter more fun, ways to keep communication flowing, and ways to pass on your values to the next generation. It is sad to hear parents talk fearfully about the future, especially the teenage years, as if they are to be dreaded. We hope you can enjoy these years as some of the best of your lives, filed with memories that you can revisit for ever.

Finally, although this book has been a combined project, for the sake of simplicity we have used the first person singular. This means the text is written in Ian's words, however, Mary's editing skills, research and wide knowledge of the subject are woven into every paragraph.

Ian and Mary Grant

Chapter 1

Your daughter's future starts now

> If you have the chance at parenthood, look upon it with a sense of mystery and awe. You are given the joy of watching life afresh, and the chance to help another being take flight into the riches and mystery of life. The very clay of which our world is made is for a brief moment placed in your hands.
>
> **— Kent Nerburn,** Simple Truths

I've just ordered woodworking plans for a small girl's doll's house, complete with miniature furniture and electric lighting. It will be my second woodworking project, following the little red rocking-horse made for a first birthday. The impetus behind this new burst of creative energy is three adorable granddaughters, all born within the last few months.

After years of building trucks and diggers for machine-orientated grandsons I am excited by the idea of these new projects. There is something about a girl that offers parents a different perspective on parenting. Her natural desire for relationships and, almost from birth, her tendency to make eye contact and respond to verbal communications rapidly begins to weave its magic in the hearts of parents and grandparents.

There are so many things to enjoy about your daughter. Her natural desire for connection and her innate ability to nurture, whether it be a doll, a pet or a friendship, mean she longs to be part of a loving family. Within her own self she has these qualities and they are your greatest ally in building strong attachments to see her through what many regard as the difficult teenage years. When you see or play with a small girl you sense the potential in her young life and you hope that she will retain her innocence and sense of self. You hope that she will keep that clear-eyed way she has of looking right into your eyes without shame or fear. Yet we hear so many stories about the ways in which our culture is toxic to girls, and about the many hurdles they will face when growing up in our individualistic and materialistic society, where so often the underlying question is 'Do you measure up?'

> Your loving consistency, and the love and interest of her wider family, are vitally important to a girl's self-esteem right through her teen years.

A concept that tends to resonate with men is that of investment banking; the idea that to be successful you have to be in for the long haul; that investing wisely at the outset and hanging in through the highs and the lows will bring about a good result in the end. There are significant parallels with this when parenting girls. The key issues are your involvement with her from the start, a resolute commitment to her no matter what, and a strong vision as to what sort of young woman you, as parents, would like to launch into the world.

In this book we have endeavoured to cover the years from the day of your daughter's birth until her late teens, with the awareness that she will need involved, loving parenting through all these years. Even as a teenager, when she is sophisticated in areas such as operating electronic devices, and appears independent and highly opinionated, because of her innate nature and biology your daughter will need intimacy and connection. Your loving consistency, and the love and interest of her wider family, are vitally important to a girl's self-esteem right through her teen years. It is not only the frontal lobes of a teenager's brain (which control risk-assessment and future thinking) that are not fully developed. Your daughter's unique female make-up means that her greatest challenge during this time will be learning to understand herself — her emotions and feelings, her physiology, and her sometimes hormonally driven energy levels. As parents we can be great allies in confirming the message in her adolescent heart that she is valuable, worthy and lovable.

This is why each stage in your daughter's life is significant, and each will provide building blocks to help her to embrace the next step healthily. The years preceding adolescence are so important. If she goes into her teenage years with only her good looks, she will be in deep trouble. During the middle years of school you have a window of opportunity to communicate and connect with her and help her develop skills. Your daughter will be keen to know what is right and wrong. She is Okay with black and white, with rules, and for a few years she will really enjoy being part of the family and learning about and taking on board its values and principles.

Often during these years girls are full of confidence and willing to try a whole range of new physical challenges. This is your opportunity for family camping holidays, excursions of all sorts, tramps, as well as family stories, traditions and discussions around the dinner table. You need to capitalise on this time. It is the equivalent in white-water rafting of the quiet part of the river when you have time to coach 'rookie rafters' in all the skills they will need before you get to the rapids. It is when you would teach them about how to paddle, the best way to handle the tricky bits, and about teamwork. The goal you have in mind is that the rapids will be an enjoyable challenge and a test of character, not a disaster area.

A parent's role

Your role is really to be an encourager, to send your daughter into her teenage years with a 'full emotional tank'; with the affection and approval she needs as well as the skills and interests that will keep her connected in different ways with others. Your messages of approval and wisdom should fill her memory bank, giving her a resilience that comes from knowing she has been prepared well with the skills she will need. You will need to provide her with boundaries about her behaviour within the family and about how she allows others to treat her. Most of all, if she learns from you that she can play after she has done what she is expected to do as a family member, then she will have the foundation for good EQ — emotional intelligence. No matter how many *Baby Einstein* videos your daughter has watched, if she does not have the basic building blocks of empathy and self-discipline her life will lack a framework and heart. EQ is the greatest gift your good parenting will secure for her.

The future for girls

Girls growing up today have so many options. The doors to just about any career are open to them, and society tends to support both their equality and their autonomy. Educationally, girls have opportunities that no other generation has enjoyed and, according to all reports, they are achieving academic success above that of their male peers. At the same time, however, there are particular challenges that are unique to the technologically saturated age into which this generation of girls has been launched.

In his book *The Wonder of Girls*, Michael Gurian suggests that the individualised, materialistic culture in which we live actually fights against a girl's need for intimacy and connection. Sadly, at the same time, our society takes less care to maintain the boundaries that should protect them.

The age of innocence is dead

Richard Lander, a Hollywood producer and the father of three young girls, a decade or so ago developed the first internet filter system, called max.com. Lander concluded, from what he saw happening in Hollywood, that the 'age of innocence' was dead. Even then, he said, there were a million paedophiles surfing the internet at any one time. More than a third of all traffic on the internet is pornography, and the largest group of accessors of pornography is 12- to 17-year-old boys. This means that girls are growing up in a society where there is a far greater tendency for men and boys to have a one-dimensional view of women, and where there is a proportion of boys who believe that women actually like the sort of demeaning activity portrayed in pornographic images.

The pervasiveness of pornography has exploded with the internet, and we parents need to adjust our vigilance accordingly.

It is not just the internet: all branches of the media expose even young girls to a wide range of adult concepts. Long before they are ready, girls (and their parents) face challenges and decisions about drugs, alcohol and sex. Our culture has pushed the fast-forward button for girls, and some suffer terribly from being prematurely accelerated into a risky and unprotected adolescence.

Since society is doing less for girls' welfare, parents need to do more. We need to be *more* vigilant and take a *more* proactive role in creating a childhood for our girls in which they will thrive.

Fortunately, the best response to all these new challenges is the time-proven formula of parental love and coaching. The basics of parenting girls are still the same as they have always been. Parents need to be both advisors and cheerleaders. We need to make sure that from their earliest days we give our daughters quality time, physical closeness and warm, loving eye-contact.

The great thing about raising our daughters is that we don't have to do it all on our own. Though Mums and Dads will always be the major influences in their lives, many adult women point to the powerful influence of other role models as they were growing up. Grandparents, uncles and aunts, coaches, Girl Guide leaders and teachers can all influence girls and inspire them to go for it and to take on hurdles rather than avoid them.

> We need to be *more* vigilant and take a *more* proactive role in creating a childhood for our girls in which they will thrive.

When we visited our nine-week-old granddaughter in London recently I was amazed at her concentration as she sat on my lap and I read to her. I had to compete with Grandma, who is an amazing baby whisperer, and I was delighted to discover once again the truth of the natural tendency of little girls to respond to verbal connections. She seemed to enjoy the tones and rhythm of my voice (as well as the puzzling pictures!) as I read one of my favourite books — Lynley Dodd's *Hairy Maclary from Donaldson's Dairy* — and it became our little ritual. Even at that age she tuned in.

From the start, plenty of conversation, emotional availability and fun will provide a backdrop for your daughter to explore the world and build confidence in her own perceptions.

Give your daughter security

> The kind of people that a baby grows up amongst will greatly affect the shape and the wiring of its mental faculties. Is the family environment relaxed or aggressive, quiet or lively, funny or deadly serious? The baby's brain responds and grows accordingly. Early in its life the adrenaline thermostat — the amount of adrenaline it is accustomed to — is set to handle what is a normal level of stress for that family.
>
> **— Steve Biddulph,** Raising Babies

Be the big person who communicates confidence and creates structure and warmth in your home. One of the key conclusions in a 10-year study led by Dr Burton White of Harvard University was that the greatest influence in building good minds in young children was parents who excelled at three key functions. They were superb organisers and designers of their child's environment; they permitted short, focused interruptions so they could comfort, convey information and answer questions; and they were firm in discipline while simultaneously showing great affection.

Never undervalue the significant role you have as a parent. Whether society recognises it or not, your contribution is indispensable in growing capable, loving adults.

The foundations are simple

A tiny baby's survival depends on her symbiotic relationship with her mother. A child who is badly nurtured will suffer from a fear that the relationship will fail. She will fear that she will not survive if she is not 'plugged into' this person. That insecurity carries over into adult life, and unhealthy, dependent relationships from this type of neurotic fear and neediness often become generational.

Fortunately you do not need a million dollars or a PhD in child psychology to meet all your daughter's needs. You just need time and your natural love and willingness to be a parent.

We recently watched a documentary in which a childhood expert was called in to help parents whose daughter of 18 months was a chronic non-sleeper. Several experts had already been consulted, and the parents had concluded that the child was so intelligent she was always on the alert, and so did not sleep. After observing the family dynamics for several days the experienced, motherly psychologist who had been called in concluded that, 'Yes, this child is very bright, and she is on alert because she is anxious. She knows that her parents are not confident in being the big people — they don't seem to know what to do — and so she is not convinced that everything is safe if she goes to sleep.'

The counsellor's advice was simple. Create a regular routine in which there is predictability and order, thereby reassuring your little one that everything is as it should be. The simple routines of dinner, playtime, bath, story and bedtime were the key to this child feeling secure and sleeping peacefully. Within a few weeks everything was different, and Mum and Dad had begun to grow in stature as they accepted their role as the big people.

hot tip ✪

✪ Have a dream about the sort of young woman you would like to launch into the world. 'See' her in her late teens as a self-assured, optimistic, adventurous, generous, honest and loving adult.

✪ Remember your home is not a democracy. Eating vegetables is not open to an equal vote, neither is going to school, or what your children do on the computer.

✪ As your daughter heads into her teenage years there will be more negotiated decisions as you capitalise on the trust you have built up and offer her the respect she craves. But you will still protect her by allowing only age-appropriate decisions – by not offering her more freedom than her maturity can handle. To see her fly solo and coach her towards self-reliance is your ultimate goal.

in summary ✏

WHAT GIRLS NEED TO CREATE A GREAT FUTURE
Girls need:

- To be brought up by someone who is crazy about them.
- To be part of a loving family.
- Parents with a strong vision of what sort of young woman they want to launch into the world.
- Lots of warmth and fun, but also routine and predictability.
- A parent who will be the big person from the start.
- A parent who will be there for the long haul.

Chapter 2

Am I welcome in the world?

Both mother and baby need to get to know each other by being responsive in each other's presence and learning to decipher each other's language . . . This is our very first love relationship. The patterns of this dance will be the blueprint on which other relationships are built.

— **Mary Sutton,** *child psychotherapist*

Early interactions are crucial. Children smile from their early days. They even smile when they are sick. When parents see them smiling, the tendency to smile back is instinctive . . . As long as there are cuddles, laughing and engaging in other close, intimate behaviour, the scene is set for a good childhood.

-- **Professor Hugh Foot,** *specialist in child psychology and social development, University of Strathclyde*

If the theme of brokenness, distrust, separation enters into her primal relationship with her parents, the devastation will reverberate into the depths of her soul and identity.

— **Janelle Hallman,** *therapist*

A m I welcome in the world? Is there a place for me? Have I got permission to be here?

Every child asks these questions. Every baby girl wants to know, am I acceptable and am I lovable? We must tell her that she is.

It is a psychological law that we need to be loved into being. From their earliest interactions, the comfort and bonding a parent offers a baby provides the emotional recorder deep inside her with messages about her worth and value. Even before a baby is born, she hears the comforting rhythm of her mother's heartbeat and, scientists now tell us, she also recognises her father's.

Early bonding or attachment gives a baby the beginnings of a sense of self. For nine months she has listened to her mother's heartbeat alongside her own, and her mother's voice is familiar and reassuring. Humans do not have the innate instincts of other animals. Even other mammals can go looking for their mother and their food source, but a new baby cannot.

This obvious physical neediness is only the tip of the iceberg when we consider what a new baby needs from a parent. It is the stroking and talking and cuddling that actually sequence your baby's brain and her emotional memory. A healthy mother pours love and life into her baby — she gently strokes the outline of her newborn, and in this way lets her know that she is welcome, is gorgeous and gives her a sense of 'being'. And this responsive type of parenting provides a way of getting to know your baby, learning to be open to her cues and establishing her sense of well-being. It is the basis of helping your daughter 'feel right', and when a child feels right she is more likely to want to please her parents and therefore to learn to act right and to be a joy to those around her.

Making the right connections

A newborn's brain is unfinished in many ways, and it is her parents' loving interactions that wire her malleable brain for the future. A baby's brain grows by two-thirds after she is born, and to do this it needs the right stimulation. A baby only grows the right parts and wires up the right connections if we provide the right experiences at the right time. And fortunately these tend to be the experiences that happen normally in a loving family where parents sing, talk and play with their little one and offer her the calm predictability of a loving home. A baby's brain is especially sensitive to the emotional tone of her surroundings. So talk to your daughter naturally as you go about changing and feeding her; chat about mundane things and tell her where you are going and what you are doing. This is all reassuring and comforting to her.

Among some of the amazing discoveries of neuroscience over the past decade is the fact that 11 million neuron pathways develop each second in an infant's brain — you could say that parents are literally co-creating galaxies of neuroconnections with their children. Caressing a baby lowers a stress hormone that is known to damage the developing brain. And evidence now shows that attentive caregiving even influences DNA production during the first year of a human's life.

These neuroconnections play an important role in the years that follow. Apparently they affect a person's ability to lead a satisfying life, to form healthy relationships, and to make ethical decisions. Tragically, many parents still think that a young baby only needs to be fed, kept warm and have her nappies changed. They miss the vital fact that it is their presence and comforting words that lay down in this pre-verbal time their daughter's ability to be optimistic, to think logically and to feel good about herself.

Trust and abandonment are the issues for your baby in the first year of her life. Our brains are a bit like wet concrete — if we register deep in our pre-verbal memory that we are not wanted, have been abandoned or are not safe, it is very hard to erase these effects in later life. If a baby's needs, cues and signals are responded to promptly, consistently and lovingly, she learns that the world can be relied upon and is predictable. Trust is built and attachment grows as both the new mother and her baby experience their relationship as emotionally and physically enjoyable.

> Tell your daughter she is lovely otherwise she will spend the rest of her life trying to prove she is capable.
>
> **– Drs John and Agnes Sturt,** Created for Love

> ## hot tip ✪
>
> ✪ A soothing routine and your familiar presence are important for your baby. So are chatting and smiles, music, dancing and things to touch and look at, especially your family's faces.
>
> ✪ It is very important that a new mother has lots of support. Her well-being will be reflected in her baby's feelings of worth.

In his 21-year study at Otago University, in which more than a thousand children were traced from birth to the age of 21, Dr Phil Silva concluded that the things that matter to young children don't necessarily relate to wealth or having all the baby gear that is peddled to new parents these days. On the contrary, he suggested that 'poor circumstances and adversity can be overcome by good parenting'. Dr Silva concluded that it is important to focus on just three basics if a young child is to thrive: care must be consistent; the early experience of the child should be rich; and children need to be loved.

None of these basics cost money, and they can be incorporated into your home and lifestyle with simplicity. So sing and dance with your baby and involve her in your daily life. Keep her with you as you move from room to room, talk to her as you go about your tasks, let her watch you and touch different textures like the wool of a lamb, dried leaves and sand at the beach. Soothing and cuddling, as well as outings in the buggy or visits to the zoo, all make up the beginnings of a rich childhood.

Enjoy your baby!

Don't think of time caring for your young child as wasted moments away from your career or workplace. Think of it rather as a special time, when as you nurture your baby's earliest feelings about herself you also have time to nurture yourself. If you can see this season in your life as a time to enjoy a simpler rhythm of life and perhaps to pursue friendships, creative activities or some active sport, then both you and your daughter will benefit.

The smile on a mother's face reassures her daughter that the world is a good place. A baby really doesn't see herself as separate from her mother. Until those more feisty months around two years of age, when she is naturally and healthily breaking away, and she discovers the words 'no', 'me', 'mine' and 'I do it', she will look to you to tell her who she is and what she is worth.

If you have to make sacrifices to be with your daughter in the first three years of her life, they will be sacrifices well worth making. This is a vital time in which to be available to reassure and protect her, to build strong attachments and to really get to know your daughter.

> All of us, from the cradle to the grave, are happiest when life is organised as a series of excursions, long or short, from the secure base provided by our attachment figures.
> — **John Bowlby**, *psychiatrist and father of attachment theory*

During a recent talk to a group of professionals on a very popular subject, work–life balance and parenting, I was a little bit on tenterhooks because many of those in the audience came from a profession that specialises in adversarial skills. After I had presented my talk I was joined by a group of three professional women, all of whom happened to be pregnant. One of the women commented, 'We really found that worthwhile, and reinforced our decision to take substantial time off after the arrival of our babies.' One of the women, who was very pregnant, said she was planning to take three years off after observing her more senior colleagues. She described one senior partner in her firm as feeling isolated from her two rebellious teenagers. 'She has had them in daycare since they were born, and now regrets the years in which nannies spent more time with her children than she did.'

With all the research that is now available concerning the first three years of a child's life, much of it reinforcing the significance of those years for bonding and attachment as well as brain development, it is unfortunate that professional women still feel so much pressure to get back to work so soon. If your daughter has the gift of your presence for the first two to three years of her life, this may be more significant for her future welfare than the high school she attends. This is a message young parents rarely hear these days, as we rush mothers back to work and minimise their value to their children and to the nation.

The consensus among child experts is that the secret of raising confident, loving and happy children is developing strong parent–child bonds, and the foundation for those bonds is laid down in the first months and years. It is what is called sensitive availability. As Michael Gurian notes in his book *Boys and Girls Learn Differently*, 'A child's brain needs bonding and attachment to fully grow and learn; without attachment it does not grow well — behaviourally, psychologically or intellectually.'

If you do need to use childcare in the first two years of your daughter's life, look for a caregiving arrangement that will allow you to have as much involvement as possible with your child and will entail minimal transitions. Every transition tends to cause anxiety for a small baby. If possible, arrange for daycare in your own home. A loving grandma or a situation where you share caregiving with one other family is better for young babies than a large daycare; babies are able to relate to only a few adults and need one consistent, familiar person to whom they can attach.

hot tip ✪

✪ If you don't have to, don't feel pressured to rush back to full-time employment and leave your young baby for long periods of time in care. Maybe you can choose less lofty lifestyle goals for a few years in order to take pressure off yourself.

The Circle of Security

The Circle of Security is a project that aims to help parents who in their own developmental history may have had little experience of trust and confidence in another. It is designed to give them the tools to parent their children in a way that will build strong attachments and sensitive responsiveness. The rationale behind the Circle of Security is that when children feel safe they are wired to be interested in their world and go out to explore. Yet while they are exploring, children look to their caregivers to act as a secure base. Sometimes they want their parents to be with them by watching, sometimes they need help, and sometimes they want their parents to enjoy or even delight in their play. While exploring, children will inevitably need to come back to be closer to their parent at some stage, because they may need comfort, help with their feelings, protection or an experience of shared delight. Children look to their caregivers to be a support and a safe haven.

The two principles for parents that are reinforced by the Circle of Security are:

- Always be bigger, stronger, wiser and kind.
- Whenever possible follow your child's need. Whenever necessary take charge.

On their website, www.circleofsecurity.com, the programme's developers say:

> Sometimes when parents try to take charge and act bigger and stronger they sacrifice being kind and become mean and harsh. Parents who act this way often believe they must become aggressive and evoke fear to have the respect of their child. Other parents, when they try to be kind, give up being bigger and stronger, abdicate their leadership, and allow the child to run the relationship. It is an ongoing challenge for all parents to be simultaneously bigger, stronger and kind and to have the wisdom to understand a child's need for security rests on the parent's ability to provide this all-important function.

They quote child psychologist Dr Karlen Lyons-Ruth, who says, 'A parent who can provide a secure base and safe haven for a child allows the child to develop a "psychological immune system":

> While your immune system does not guarantee you will never get

sick, it does provide the crucial mechanism for healing when you do. Children with secure attachments have caregivers they can go to in times of stress who will help them calm themselves and solve problems. Evidence from a number of researchers shows that children who are secure do better across a broad range of developmental outcomes.

This is a 'difference that makes a difference', and one that caregivers can do something about.

However, the real spin-off of caring for your child in those early years is that you as a mother or father will fall in love with your child. Relative to mothers of insecure children, mothers of preschool-age 'secure' children display more positive moods, delight in and enjoyment of their children, non-intrusive play and teaching, and provide a relaxed home atmosphere.

In other words, being the big person means being kind, loving and warm but firm, and providing for physical needs along with being emotionally available. If your toddler tries to boss you, for example, by demanding that you come with her to play on the slide when you are finishing your coffee, you could go with her immediately, if you don't want the rest of your drink. Alternatively, you could say, 'Yes, Mummy will come and play with you on the slide when I have finished my coffee; in the meantime you can sit here by me or you can play by yourself on the slide while I finish my coffee and watch you.' You are still giving her emotional support even if you cannot come immediately she wants you.

What we now know about the first three years of a baby's life is that it provides the foundation for her future life's potential. So as much as possible enter into the joy of raising your daughter. Enrol her in music and movement classes, take her to the library, talk to her not just in monosyllables but in full, complex sentences and, if you want to, learn baby sign language. You will be surprised at how much your daughter is absorbing and how she will respond, and you will be building into her reservoir of language your own understanding of and delight in this little person.

The importance of confident parents

Children gain security from their parents' confidence. A regular routine and a confident parent make all the difference to how a child feels about the world. Your small daughter will feel secure if she knows what is going to happen, and that there are two adults who are in charge.

If a small person subconsciously thinks, 'I am in charge,' then the second question that follows must be, 'What will happen if I get into trouble, because the big people don't seem to know what to do?'

hot tip ✪

- ✪ Find support networks and ways to build a life that will nurture you as a person while you are parenting your baby.
- ✪ Avoid the temptation to put your child in front of television. Plan some highlights in your week that both you and your baby can look forward to. Walk with the buggy and a friend in parks or by beaches, and when you are ready join a tennis club, or book group, or a mothers' group, so that you have structure and 'markers' to look forward to in your week.
- ✪ Play with your baby for a few minutes each day. Build something with her, play peek-a-boo, teach her a new skill or just enjoy her.
- ✪ Touch and hold your baby regularly. Use expressive faces when you are talking to her. Play wordplay games and action songs. Sing lullabies.

in summary ✎

WHAT A NEW BABY NEEDS
Babies and very young children need:

- ➾ Secure bonding and attachment – trust your instincts as a mother and enjoy your child.
- ➾ Lots of stimulation – sing, talk and play with your little one.
- ➾ A calm and predictable environment.
- ➾ A safe haven to return to.
- ➾ Parents who are confident and 'in charge'.

Chapter 3

The nature of girls

Every parent knows that on a rainy day, boys will play games like
'urban commando' or 'terrorise the cat', whereas girls will play
wedding days, princesses or tea parties . . . The fact of the matter
is that girls will play relational games.

— **John Eldredge,** Wild at Heart

She is feeling, hearing, smelling more than he is and enjoying
those senses; and she is creating an interior world that is much
more sense- and contact-laden than is a boy's.

— **Michael Gurian,** The Wonder of Girls

We need to be nice to Jassy, even though she talks so much.
That's just girls — they need to talk a lot . . . My mummy talks all
the time, but she's really nice.

— **Sam,** 7

Girls are hardwired for delight, relationship and connection. By
nature your daughter is drawn to connect with others.

Girls are relational to the core. Unless there has been some
trauma or disruption of attachment, parents tend to discover this from a
girl's earliest days. Your daughter's joy in your company, and her ability
to articulate her feelings even as a small child, may surprise you. A small

daughter who runs to greet you at the end of the day, sharing a story about her latest 'new' friend, or who insists on wearing her tutu and gumboots to kindergarten, wants your approval and she wants to connect. She needs to hear from you a resounding 'Yes, you're lovely, and I am glad you're my daughter.'

We all know that there is something unique about the nature of girls, and it is right to celebrate their emerging femininity. Enjoy your daughter. If you can delight in her, know how to meet her genuine needs and be the big person who takes charge when she needs you to, then you have mastered the art of parenting a girl. If your eyes light up when she enters the room you are meeting her deepest need for approval and affection. When she arrives in the kitchen with flowers she has just picked for you from the garden (or maybe your not-yet-ripe tomatoes!), if you can look past the dirt on the floor or the lost salad, and see the love and desire to connect from the heart, then you will give your daughter the roots she needs to thrive.

While not taking away from the idea that girls can and should be encouraged to take part in all the activities their brothers enjoy, excellent research is now telling us that many of the stereotypes about girls are true, not because of social conditioning, but because they are biologically programmed. We have all noticed that at playgroup the 'Wendy house' has more girls than boys playing in it, and the retailers who fill shelves with dolls, tea-sets and fairy costumes are very aware of this difference. A little girl's bedroom is likely to be all about princesses in waiting — Cinderella, Snow White or Sleeping Beauty. I love the way Catherine O'Dolan described it in an article run by our local newspaper, titled 'In Praise of Tutus': 'Is it something in the genes? Are little girls really pre-programmed to want something floaty that just cries out "I'm a girl and I love it!" . . . If she is in a bad mood or feeling blue, I'm the first to prescribe that instant pick me up — head to the dress up box and put on your tutu. I defy anyone not to summon up at least a pouty smile when surrounded by ample amounts of frothy netting and a little girl.' And yes — it is right to reassure her that she makes a lovely fairy, princess or Snow White.

A girl's natural drive for intimacy and connection is the essence of her nature. Her friendships will always be a source of pleasure and support, and sometimes pain, because of the way she is. Playing with dolls occurs in every culture, and the desire to nurture is as natural to girls as wrestle-play is to little boys. We now know that if you work with her nature, rather than denying it, you will allow her the freedom to be anything she wants to be. Children who are very secure in their gender identity have higher self-esteem and tend to have the ability to move happily, without a sense of inferiority, in mixed situations.

Every cell in a girl's body is wired differently from a boy's, programmed to develop along a different path. As John and Stasi Eldredge, authors of the book *Captivating*, say, 'While little boys are killing one another in mock battles little girls are negotiating relationships. A woman longs to be desired.'

We also know that as she heads into puberty the secret world of a girl is influenced in many subtle ways by her hormones. One psychologist recently suggested that we are coming out of the Dark Ages of parenting — the years when gender studies were driven by theories based on assumptions about the power of social conditioning, which don't necessarily hold up in the light of new research — and it is now much more widely accepted that biology plays a significant role in gender bias and wiring.

> Children who are very secure in their gender identity have higher self-esteem and tend to have the ability to move happily, without a sense of inferiority, in mixed situations.

In the last decade or so, using advanced scanning techniques, scientists have uncovered some of the secrets of girls' brains. In *The Wonder of Girls*, Michael Gurian explains that the female brain is coded to grow more quickly from right to left than the male, so girls are more in touch with their feelings than small boys: 'The left hemisphere, where most language takes place, develops earlier in girls . . . the female brain is coded to secrete more serotonin than the male. Higher serotonin secretion is directly related to greater impulse control . . . One- to three-year-old girls will tend to be physically calmer than same age boys . . . the female brain also secretes more oxytocin than a male's and oxytocin secretion directly relates to play with care-objects or babies. Girls of any age play with dolls and other care-objects more than boys do.'

Studies have shown that in simple terms the wiring of the retina of the eye to the brain is different in girls to that in boys — the effect of this is that when girls draw pictures they prefer colours such as red, orange, green and beige, whereas boys prefer colours such as black, grey, silver and blue. These are actual physiological differences arising from the thickness of the retina, the number of the cells known as P cells and M cells, and how the retina connects to the brain.

As Dr Leonard Sax states in his fascinating book *Why Gender Matters*, 'Sex differences in toy preferences start to make more sense once you understand this research. A richly textured doll will be more appealing than a moving truck if your system favours the P cells as is the case in females.' (For more on the physiological gender differences in babies see www.genderdifferences.org)

In their pictures small girls tend to draw nouns, whereas boys draw verbs. Little girls' pictures are much more likely to be about family and people, whereas little boys will draw rockets and machines. Girl babies seem to be born pre-wired to be interested in relationships and faces, while boys are pre-wired to be more interested in moving objects. Girls respond earlier and more strongly to the human face and the human voice. They smile sooner.

In a study at Cambridge University, more than a hundred babies were videotaped and their eye movements analysed as they responded to a variety of stimulants, including a young woman's face and a mobile. The researchers, found that the girls were more interested in the face of the young woman, whereas the boys were more than twice as likely to prefer the mobile. Following extended studies, the researchers concluded that they had proven 'beyond reasonable doubt' that sex differences in social interest are, in part, biological in origin.

Girls and boys actually do see and hear differently. Girls see much more detail, and they have better hearing. The latter is particularly interesting

— a girl's hearing is far more sensitive than a boy's, and girls sometimes think that their father or a male teacher is talking too loudly. Generally, girls are also stronger in verbal fluency. They are more empathetic, caring and emotionally expressive than boys.

We also know that women are more sensitive to different degrees of temperature, different kinds of touch, tones of voice, odours, and the like. For a good summary of the many differences between men and women that are now known to be rooted in biology and brain differences, see *Brain Sex: The Real Difference Between Men and Women*, by Anne Moir and David Jessel.

Girls are complex

A lot happens internally for a girl that may not be reflected externally. Girls display less anger than boys, but more fear, distress and embarrassment. This is where wise parenting can make a difference to your daughter's development. Emotional support and a listening ear enable a child to negotiate stressful situations much more healthily. A loving adult who is able to interpret a negative situation will give her daughter perspective, and the ability to avoid personalising what has happened and relating it to her worth or lack of it.

You need to ensure that your daughter knows you love her, and to reassure her about this constantly. Have a family code that communicates this message. When you are walking and holding her hand, give her five squeezes and tell her it means 'Do you love me?' Then show her how to squeeze your hand back, meaning 'Yes I do!' Next squeeze her hand twice: 'How much?' She squeezes yours once, which means 'Zillions!' This then becomes a code between you, which either of you can instigate and enjoy at any time, and in many situations. It can be helpful right into your daughter's teenage years, when she has become more oppositional, less communicative, and highly sensitive about what her friends think.

hot tip ✪

✪   Have some unique family ways of letting your daughter know you love her. This might be a bedtime ritual of butterfly kisses, or a special song you sing, like 'I'll love you forever', or carrying her to bed a different way each night.

CONNECT WITH YOUR DAUGHTER

A dad told me recently that he drives his 14-year-old daughter and her friends to school every day in his plumber's van, and his daughter has asked him to drop them off a street away from the school gate so as not to embarrass her. He says the girls very rarely if ever engage him in conversation — usually it is just a nod or a grunt of farewell as they hop out. As their daughter is only 14, he and his wife maintain firm rules about the times at which she is allowed to be out unsupervised. For example, they had refused her permission to attend a rock concert with just her 14-year-old friends. In consultation with the other parents they had offered alternatives, such as one set of parents accompanying the girls, but this had been turned down. In consequence, there was a distinct coldness in the young girl's responses to her parents for a day or two.

During this time the dad was still driving the girls to school, and so had the challenge of the group showing some unease in his company. He decided, however, that he was the adult in the situation, and so he continued as normal, refusing to buy in to the emotional distance the girls had created. He had heard me speak at a seminar about the importance, as a man, of knowing how to conduct a conversation with girls. I had explained that we men tend to converse about the facts, while as a rule girls want to expand, are interested in feelings, and often want more detail. As men, we tend to finish conversations too soon with both our wives and our daughters.

My tip had been to imagine that you have a tennis ball in your hand; when you are talking to your daughter, 'see' the questions and responses as the ball going backward and forwards between you. The skill, however, is to figuratively not put the tennis ball in your pocket, but to let her end the conversation. In this way she will feel that you have really 'talked' to her. With this information in mind the father decided to take on the challenge of chatting with these teenagers. He asked them their opinion of a band he knew they were keen on, and within a few minutes his daughter had turned around from talking to her friends in the back seat and had begun to talk to him, answering his questions and giving her opinion. Then, as they neared the school, she said, 'Oh Dad, you can drop us off at the school gate if you like.' He drew up at the gate, quietly pleased that the atmosphere had warmed, and as she got out of the van he leant over and said, 'I may seem as if I'm being tough over this concert, but it is because you are very precious to us and it is our responsibility to make sure you are safe!' His daughter pulled away, but a moment later he felt her hand on his arm, then a squeeze from their old code, 'Do you love me?' He knew he had connected!

Conversation and connection can make a huge difference

Build strong bonds of love and availability with your daughter — they will stand you in good stead as she grows. Read to her and talk to her. Let her read to you.

Build into your schedule times of focused attention, like five minutes on the end of her bed before lights out, or a cup of Milo when she arrives home. Ask her about the best bits of her day and the worst bits, and give her the gift of your adult listening and wisdom.

Let her have her day interpreted through the loving maturity of your adult perspective. Children are good observers but poor interpreters. Because of her desire for good relationships, she is more likely to be upset by things people say than perhaps her brothers would be. She will need you to interpret situations for her: 'Darling, this was only pretend,' or 'This wasn't about your value or worth, this was about Janie feeling yuck and saying something nasty.'

Just for a treat, tell your daughter, 'If you are in bed before I count to 10 we can have two minutes' talk in the dark.' She will love it.

Occasionally pick up your daughter and her siblings out of bed in their pyjamas and take them out for an ice cream or some other 'conspiratorial treat'. My favourite is loading them in the car to go to a takeaway for a milkshake!

hot tip ✪

✪ Bring home surprises, and have lots of celebrations. Make speeches to her on her birthday. Let each family member make a positive speech about what they love most about her.

By doing these things you are creating for her the building blocks of the important social connections she needs. Dr JoAnn Deak, in her book *Girls Will Be Girls*, suggests that family, focus and fun will build a good life for her. A strong family, surrounded wherever possible by the wider family, and later her involvement in some interest outside the family, will build the strong connections and community she needs.

Girls and risks

You need to teach your daughter how to take smart risks. It is not unusual, when a boy is injured while playing sport, for his father to ask the doctor when he will be able to play again, whereas when a daughter has been injured, the parents will often ask if the doctor thinks she should give up sport. Staying involved in sport is so important for girls. It gives them another social group in which they belong, it is important for their physical fitness and well-being, and it develops their coordination skills. Unfortunately girls often drop out of sport if they think they are not good enough, or if they don't have a special friend in the team. Ensure you have a family rule that goes something like this: your children must all play a summer sport and a winter sport, but they are allowed to choose which sport they play. In this way they know they have an element of control, albeit an age-appropriate one.

Smart risks are risks that can be managed if things go wrong. If your daughter has a more cautious nature than her siblings, let her practise on the small slide at the playground until her confidence has been built up, and let her venture out with you into the gentle waves, but don't accept avoidance because she is a girl.

Your daughter's basic need is to feel safe. Without scaring her, teach her why something is safe, or what is necessary to make it safe.

The other secret quality – a girl's hormones

As the years go by, increasing biochemical research is unveiling the complexity and wonder of a girl's physiology as well as the interplay of hormones with her brain and emotional development. In *The Wonder of Girls*, Michael Gurian comments, 'Hormones are getting increased credit for female existence, success, happiness, self-esteem and quality of life — that's how powerful they are.'

In simple scientific terms, hormones are the boss molecules that tell the brain and body what to do.

Hormones are the agents of change not just for a few things but for everything, and they don't just change your daughter from a girl to a woman; they are in many

> It is a normal part of a girl's hormonal cycle to feel low, depressed or emotional at times, and she needs understanding and knowledge so that she can map these times and handle them.

ways the woman herself.

Traditionally this message of female biology has been handed down through the lines of female knowledge from mother to daughter. To some extent, however, it has been lost in our individualistic age where so much has been explained in terms of social conditioning, and answers have often been looked for in medication. It is a tragedy to see young teenage girls being put on medication as a first resort when suffering from mild depression, when very often they would respond to a deeper understanding of their hormonal make-up and cycle. It is a normal part of a girl's hormonal cycle to feel low, depressed or emotional at times, and she needs understanding and knowledge so that she can map these times and handle them. From the age of nine or 10 these hormones are going to start affecting her.

Your daughter's diet is especially important at puberty. Not only is it important to set up healthy eating patterns for the future, but the protein and vitamins she eats give her the fuel she needs to cope during the changes that are occurring. Sadly, this is the time when so many girls get into diets, junk food or both. By encouraging diet change, along with an understanding of her hormonal make-up, psychologists trained in hormonal diagnosis have helped parents change their teenage daughters from being troubled and depressed into balanced young women who succeed both at school and in their social development.

There is now a strong consensus that self-esteem is linked not only to capability and a sense of confidence but also to her hormonal cycle. A girl's understanding of her own nature and biology, and the knowledge of how to live in harmony with that reality, affects her resilience markedly.

In her book *The Female Brain*, neuropsychiatrist Louann Brizendine argues that women have often suffered when differences between men's and women's brains have been ignored. 'When these patients tried to talk to their own doctors or psychiatrists about how their hormones were affecting their emotions they would get the "brushoff".'

Brizendine says that advances in neuro-imaging and neuro-endocrinology have begun to supply exciting insights into how women and men use their brains differently. For example, different levels of oestrogen, cortisol and dopamine can cause a female to be more stressed by emotional conflict than her male counterpart. A few unpaid bills can set off a cascade of hormones in a woman that can catapult her into a fear of impending catastrophe, a reaction triggered in men only by physical danger.

Women have 11 per cent more neurons in the area of the brain devoted to emotions and memory than men do. It is because they have more 'mirror neurons' that they are also better at observing emotions in others.

The nature of girls sets them up with qualities that can give them great strengths, but the tendency to want to belong and the effect of hormones can also put them at risk in our technological, media-saturated society. For example, text bullying affects girls in particular. Because of their relational natures they will return again and again to a bullying message, wondering why someone would say something like that, and why they are not liked or accepted.

Positives for parents to build on

Understanding your daughter's nature puts you in a great position to be the parent and coach she needs. Your role in shaping her choices and goals will affect her achievements to an even greater degree than her innate abilities. Her family's good expectations of her, your support and your efforts to weave her strong wider family and social networks, will help build her self-esteem and moral development.

Many of the qualities discussed above mean that girls are more ready for school than boys. Girls tend to read and speak better than boys, and generally suit the cooperative style of learning common in schools today. By and large the changes to education over the last few decades have benefited girls immensely, as they are more skilled in group discovery and discussion-style learning.

Read with your daughter and stay in touch. As she grows, read the set books she has for English or history. Over family meal times, discuss and debate their merits and perspectives. As she bounces up against your ideas and values, and has permission to think for herself, she will consolidate her ideas and retain her 'voice'.

Over the last generation or so girls have been encouraged to study languages rather than physics and maths, because it was believed that was where their strengths lay. Now, however, most educationalists agree that girls succeed equally in every subject. For girls it is the *style* in which these subjects are taught that matters, and for this reason girls do tend to succeed better at single-sex schools.

Action lab ➤➤

HOW TO WORK WITH YOUR DAUGHTER'S NATURE

Girls have a 'relational' nature, so connect in ways that make her feel understood:

➤➤ *Make books for your daughter with photos of her extended family (faces especially attract her). Name all the family members, or tell her something about one of them. Use the photos to teach her something – like pointing out all their noses, or counting the number of people.*

➤➤ *Bring home surprises – they say to your daughter, 'I was thinking about you.'*

➤➤ *Sit on the floor in her room and ask your three-year-old the names of her dolls and stuffed toys.*

➤➤ *Invite your small daughter on a date – a meal on her own with you every few months – and continue this as a tradition.*

➤➤ *Take her with you when you go to the hardware store, the gardening centre, or to fix something for Grandma.*

➤➤ *Take her fishing with you, and talk to her.*

in summary ✏

WHAT GIRLS NEED

Girls need parents who:

- Let them know they're lovely.
- Provide emotional support and a listening ear.
- Help them to interpret situations – children are good observers but poor interpreters.
- Encourage them to take smart risks.
- Help them to understand their hormonal make-up, so they can map their cycles and handle the difficult times.
- Have high expectations of them.

Chapter 4

Daughters and self-esteem

All children long for recognition and acceptance of their essence — secretly so do most adults. The insistent question inside all of us is: do you see me, not only my body, but my essence; the gifts, potential, needs, wounds, character, and quality of soul that shape me individually?

The core parenting challenge (beyond meeting a child's basic needs) is to nurture this new, emerging human identity.

— Professor Richard Whitfield, *writer and educator*

Once a child has a specific image of themselves, of their own skills, abilities and level of success, they will actually choose their activities and the degree of success in these activities, to maintain their current image of themselves ... What I am saying here is that contrary to common opinion, children generally do not work to **improve** their self-concept, but rather to **prove** it.

— Laughton King, *psychologist*, With, Not Against

My parents were great encouragers. Dad would take me fishing even when I was quite small and talk to his friends about what a great fishing buddy I was, and how good I was at it. I just thought that I was one of them and so expected to be good at it.

— **Rebecca,** *21*

We often talk about the concept of self-worth, or self-esteem, but there is some debate about what this actually means. Your daughter will tend to have an image of herself that is made up from a variety of experiences and social interactions. While the mirror you give her of her worth and value will be a foundational source of her self-image, that is not the whole story. Her self-image will also be influenced and coloured by her history, her temperament, things she has heard people say, her childish conclusions about what others have said, her natural abilities or lack of them, her perception of her own success or failure, and the things she has told herself.

In our family, our daughter, now a very warm, loving, vibrant adult, tended towards the dramatic as a child. She could be incredibly happy or sad, and she seemed to be born with the words 'Don't make me feel bad about myself' on her lips. There is no doubt that understanding something about your child's temperament, and parenting her in a way that will make her feel accepted, is a real key for parents whose child may be 'tricky' or even needy. In our daughter's case her temperament is the classic 'otter' — the entertainer who needs lots of affection, attention and approval to feel good about herself. As a teenager we loved her arrival home at the end of the day because the familiar burst of welcome would usually start with something like, 'You'll never guess what happened to me today!' And then out would tumble a story of amazing coincidences and happenings, all made more interesting by the telling!

It was later in life that I learned about personality types, and the tendency for children to thrive when given the thing they value most, like respect, control or attention. I then realised what a key this was for self-esteem. If you as a parent value doing everything the 'right' way, because your personality is more that of a 'beaver', then you may not offer your 'otter' child the sense that she is worthy. For more on personality types see chapter 8.

Healthy self-esteem is a child's armour against the challenges of everyday life. Kids who feel good about themselves, and who experience some area of competence and success, seem to have an easier time handling conflicts and resisting negative pressures. However, children who early in life draw negative conclusions about themselves are likely to live with a sort of glass ceiling in their head. As Laughton King, an experienced psychologist and parenting writer, suggests, 'Once formed, a person's self-concept is very resistant to change and may in itself limit or regulate the person's ability to perform both at school and in life generally.'

A parent's role is really to be an encourager, and to send their child into her adult years with a healthy emotional bank account, with the resources in her head and her heart to operate confidently and happily in the world. So what are these resources?

Well, they are made up of a collection of what I call 'deep knowings'. These are reassurances at the deepest level that her most basic questions — 'Am I lovable?' 'Am I acceptable?' — are answered positively, giving the sense that she belongs and that she is listened to. In other words, lots of the right sort of attention, approval from her family and friends, along with the sense that she can be proud of her own achievements and character.

> You will grow a 'can do' girl when she senses you are backing her.
>
> — **Sylvia Rimm,** *psychologist and educator,*
> *author of* See Jane Win

We often hear the saying 'When the going gets tough, the tough get going', but it would perhaps be more true to life to say that when things get tough the 'much loved' get going. When we talk about self-worth or self-esteem we are really talking about parents caring enough for their children to take the time to ensure they are well-equipped in what really matters for their future life. For a girl this means making sure she is surrounded by people who speak into her life, who love her and create a circle of strong attachments from which she can explore the world, knowing there is a place to which she can return to lick her wounds if necessary, be listened to and given some more insights or skills.

Your daughter needs to know she is loved in spite of any shortcomings. A great way to show your love each day is to send her off with encouraging words and to greet her with warmth and delight: 'Have a wonderful day; your teacher is so lucky to have you in her class'; 'Wow, you look like you've had a busy day. I've been looking forward to seeing you.'

Be your child's 'interpreter'

I have a therapist friend who is convinced that 90 per cent of his work with adults would be redundant if, years before, their parents had sat on the end of their beds and debriefed them at the end of the day. Let your daughter tell a big person about the good as well as the bad bits. Because children are good observers but poor interpreters, they will take on board things that people have said and create an identity based on how others define them. Your child doesn't need all your attention all the time, but short times of focused attention when she knows she is safe to confide anything she wishes are vital. By asking her 'What was the nicest thing that happened today?' or 'What was the yuckiest thing?' you have opened a conversation with your daughter that will help her reinterpret events from a loving adult's perspective and perhaps change any false conclusions.

Mary often says she remembers, as a child, suffering sleepless nights because she thought she had done something really bad, when an adult's reassurance would have altered her false conclusions and allayed her fears. Another friend tells how she suffered teenage depression which a counsellor traced back to her conclusion as a five-year-old that if she had been good and prayed enough the starving children of the world would have been saved.

Always finish this type of conversation with something about the day that your daughter could be thankful about, then share one thing you are thankful for.

Acceptance by loved ones is the beginning of acceptance of self

To feel deeply loved, to know that you matter, to be celebrated as a treasured member of a family, to have loving adults explain that other people's comments don't necessarily reflect the truth about your value or worth — this is the beginning of acceptance of self.

So by helping your daughter to understand the nature of the world, and giving her messages that create a sense of purpose and resilience, you are offering that elusive quality we label self-esteem. No child will grow a healthy sense of place and acceptance in the world without a loving adult to help them interpret life. Children's poor interpretations of what they observe, and their immature negative conclusions about themselves, can sometimes be life-defining. It is a loving adult who can give the wisdom of perspective and the protection of age-appropriate expectations.

It is a loving parent who will teach their child that:

- problems can be solved;
- mistakes are Okay, especially while you are still learning;
- you can think for yourself;
- you can influence others with your opinions and ideas.

When Dad says, 'Gemma, would you help me with this bolt, because you can reach in there and you're good at doing things with your hands', or 'Show me how Facebook works on the computer', or tells her, 'I'm impressed', when she fixes the chain on her bike herself, then he is building self-esteem.

The people who struggle the most in life tend to lack resources — the mental and emotional strengths that come from coaching by loving parents. They not only don't have skills to fit in with others or to handle their emotions, but they don't have the resilience that comes from parents' wise words. One girl told me about an occasion when she was sitting an important exam at university — suddenly her mind went blank, but as she began to panic she remembered her dad's words of years ago, when he had said, 'You have a good mind, Suzie.' She immediately relaxed, her recall returned and she finished the exam.

If children feel good about themselves they will have the confidence to try things, and they won't be crippled by self-doubts and shyness.

If a girl — even a naturally shy one — has had a parent coach her and set her up for success, she will have the confidence to ask for what she needs or to welcome a visitor into her home.

Attention – the right sort

We recently called on friends at their holiday bach where they were celebrating a young niece's birthday. The five-year-old watched quietly and smiled as the big cousins took us outside and showed us the 'birthday flag' they had climbed to the top of a tree to fly for her. Family tradition demanded that every child had a flag made especially for them, with their name and a design of their choosing painted on it, and this flag was faithfully flown on the front lawn on their birthday, wherever they were. So if the birthday was at the cousins' holiday bach, the flag went there. In the sunroom were the unwrapped presents and the remains of the family breakfast, and in the common area of the cottage the mothers were in the process of making the five-year-old's favourite dessert for the evening meal. I have no doubt that this little girl will have the basis for a healthy sense of self-worth.

Make sure you build positive attention into your child's life. If you catch her doing something good and praise her, maybe even stop for a quick hug, she will thrive. Look for the thing that your daughter is actually doing right, even in a tricky situation, so you can praise the part she is cooperating over and move her up the ladder towards full cooperation. For instance, if your three-year-old refuses to stay in her bed, you can tell her you will leave the door open and pop back to see how nicely she is settling, but the door will have to close if she doesn't stay in her bed. Then, within a minute or two, look into her bedroom and say something like, 'I'm just popping in to see how nicely you are staying in your bed.'

Remember that children will go for the thing that gets them their parents' attention, even bad behaviour, so make sure you take the initiative and acknowledge good behaviour.

How will she define herself?

The current generation of girls tends to have a natural confidence and sense of self during the primary-school years — but that confidence will often dissipate as they head for college. Girls growing up today are likely to play soccer, enjoy cooking, climb trees, and like dressing up, riding ponies, playing with dolls or building forts. They don't seem to be limited by straitjacket role models or stereotypical adult expectations. However, what is disconcerting about modern girls is the tendency to lose that confidence as they approach the age of 11 or 12, and to disappear into a different self. It's almost as if they become aware of how others may perceive them and the culture of thinness and body image, and begin to reinvent themselves in a way that they think is necessary to be acceptable. This is the time when we need to be especially vigilant.

Help your daughter to keep alive her dreams and to have a passion or interest that fires her enthusiasm about the possibilities of her life.

A girl needs to be able to define herself by her activities and qualities, not just her looks — if she goes into her teenage years with only her good looks, then she is in deep trouble. In *Girls Will Be Girls*, Dr JoAnn Deak suggests that self-esteem should be based on girls doing things: athletic doing, creative doing and connected doing.

Athletic doing

Athletic doing can offer so much to a girl. From her earliest years, plan physical activity with and for your girls. Have a family rule of equal outdoor physical time to couch time (time spent reading, watching TV, etc.). Organise family games of cricket, take your children out tramping, teach your daughter how to kick a ball and sink a basket, but especially motivate her by being part of and enjoying sport.

When our children were little we used to hold family races after dinner each evening in the lounge. Part of the ritual involved ensuring our daughter won some of the races, even if it meant holding her highly competitive brother back by his pyjama pants, for a second or two, when we pressed the horn to start! Fun, informal family activity will build confidence. But when she is old enough, sign her up for team sport and, as a family, support her involvement.

Girls who participate in sport develop skills in leadership, problem-solving and physical coordination. Sport adds to their reservoir of confidence and competence, and team sports create another community for them. Unfortunately, many girls drop out of sport as they enter high school. It may be because they don't see themselves as good enough, or perhaps they don't have friends in the team.

It is really important to insist your daughter stays in team sports. Apart from the ability to win and lose graciously, and the skills she will hone, the belonging created through being in the team is important. If your daughter grows different friendships through being in a sports team, then if another friendship group goes sour she will have a place to be where those relationships aren't so intrusive.

Have a family rule that each of your children must play one sport each season. Allow them to make age-appropriate choices about which sport they play, but they must see out the season. Another spin off of playing sport is that it will motivate your daughter to focus on healthy eating and getting enough sleep. All helpful in weathering the ups and downs of puberty.

Commit to some sort of exercise with your daughter. A dad I know asked his daughter to help him get in shape for a marathon. It was the catalyst for her getting off the couch and eventually becoming a long-distance runner herself.

hot tip ✪

A girl's biological make-up means that she will do much better in relation to both her health and her mood stability if she has regular exercise. Her emotional health is linked in many ways to her diet, and studies now show that exercise helps stave off depression and reduces its recurrence.

Girls are more susceptible to putting on weight through eating junk food than are boys. Because female bodies are driven by oestrogen they turn more of what they eat into fat, while a boy's testosterone system turns more into muscle. Girls also hold their stress, as it were, in the cells of their body, whereas boys act out their stress through aggression. It is therefore important to eat healthily as a family — lots of fruit, vegetables and grains, keeping fats and carbohydrates such as sugars to a minimum.

Creative doing

Creative doing — writing, dancing, singing, inventing things, and other artistic activities — is well worth encouraging. Things like making and writing cards for family and friends, or family concerts where your children practise an item to perform, all contribute to a sense of significance. Knowing that she is good at something is a real boost to your daughter's self-esteem, as is a sense of 'progress'.

If your daughter has already done a few years of music or dancing or drama before she heads off to intermediate school, she will start to identify herself as others see her — 'Emma the violinist' or 'Janie the dancer'. Every child has some talent or ability that when polished up can allow them to excel. It might be artistic, academic or sporting, or it might be something like an ability to make friends or make people laugh.

Get in early during the primary-school years and start cultivating your daughter's skills. Be prepared to try out a range of things. Just because you loved poetry doesn't mean your daughter will want to follow suit. Your music genes might be dormant in your daughter — perhaps they will show up in your grandchildren — but in the meantime introduce her to something else like painting or dancing. You may get clues about where your child's gifts lie early on, but chances are she will have to try a few things before it becomes clear. Remember — every child is a gifted child — it's just that their gifts are sometimes very well wrapped.

Connected doing

Connected doing — keeping up with family traditions and conversations, plus positive social activities within a group — also helps nurture feelings of connectedness and belonging. Family mealtimes around the table are not negotiable if you want to build a family and help your daughter achieve — more about this under 'Make mealtimes a highlight' in chapter 6.

Family traditions build a family culture creating the sense that 'we always do this'. Young people who don't take part in healthy family rituals and traditions often go looking for that sense of belonging inappropriately, in gangs or online.

If your family hasn't had a lot of shared traditions, then begin some with the current generation. Think Friday-night pizza and Pictionary, or a DVD and Chinese. Birthdays, Christmas, wedding anniversaries and the end of term are all opportunities to create family traditions. One family I know have a wacky Wednesday. Their five-year-old jumps off the school bus asking 'Is it wacky Wednesday?' because she knows they do things a bit differently that day, that dinner is a surprise — sometimes served back to front, sometimes a picnic in front of the fire, sometimes a hide-and-seek meal (see page 78), and sometimes a manners meal (see page 86).

In our family we gave speeches on birthdays. This occurred during a private family birthday meal, and the rule was that everyone had to make a positive speech about the birthday person. Brothers and sisters aren't necessarily good at affirming each other, and so once a year we heard everyone say what they thought was great about their sibling or child. This is a great self-esteem builder — for the child who hears the speeches directed towards her, and for the one who gets to practise speaking publicly (if only within the family) and to speak affirmingly about another.

A teenager recently told me about her family's birthday tradition and how it had given her a real anchor when she wasn't always feeling great about herself or totally accepted by her peers. It began the night before when the whole family secretly made a banner that was hung up in the lounge. On the morning of the birthday, they would all jump into bed with Mum and Dad and open the presents, then everyone except the birthday person would go out into the kitchen, Dad would smooth the sheets and plump up the cushions like she was someone special, and they would all come back in a procession with breakfast on a tray and a 'fruit' cake, which was some sort of fruit with a candle in it!

> ## hot tip ✪
>
> 'A variety of activities and family traditions will build a meaningful life and a sense of competence,' says Dr JoAnn Deak in *Girls Will Be Girls*. 'They also provide girls with a range of friendship groups. If they already have a physical pursuit (sports, dance, fencing) before they begin high school, a creative pursuit (art, drama, gardening) and an intellectual pursuit (reading, music, writing) they are much more likely to be defined by those activities and the qualities they bring, rather than by the fact that they are slim and have the latest gear.'

What makes kids optimistic, and can we inoculate them against depression and negativity?

There has been over many years a self-esteem movement that encourages us to tell our children to feel good about themselves no matter what. However, many experts now say that the key to good self-esteem is not found in good **feelings** about ourselves but in **actions**.

Being told to feel better, when you haven't acted or done better, is not the way forward according to Dr Martin Seligman, author of *The Optimistic Child*. He suggests that when children learn helplessness it is not because bad things happen to them, it is because they think they can do nothing about those bad things. Dr Seligman describes an experiment that was carried out on dogs, in which the animals were given electric shocks; the researchers were amazed to find that even though the dogs could have moved away from the shocks they didn't, because they knew they couldn't do anything to stop the shocks. 'We found that we could cure helplessness by teaching animals that their actions had effects, and we could prevent learned helplessness by providing early experience with mastery.'

Dr Seligman determined that pessimism undermined people's ability to fight off depression, and that pessimists were more likely to give in to helplessness, putting them at greater risk of depression.

There is also research which suggests children who are inner-directed have much happier lives and better outcomes in every way than those who rely on external factors to mould their behaviour. The latter believe that chance or luck control their circumstances, whereas children who are inner-directed have strong values, goals and qualities of persistence.

All this leads to the premise that you can actually inoculate children against learned helplessness and give them the resilience to fight off depression and mental illness, in much the same way that we immunise our kids against polio or whooping cough.

In Dr Seligman's words: 'We want more for our children than healthy bodies. We want our children to have lives filled with friendship and love and high deeds. We want them to be eager to learn and be willing to confront challenges . . . And we want them to be resilient in the face of the set backs and failures that growing up brings.' The trouble with pessimism, he suggests, is that it can feel trendy, but it quickly becomes an entrenched habit of mind that leads to resignation and underachievement. We believe the current 'emo' culture is worth steering young people away from with its negative, passive and drop-out mindset.

Persistence in the face of challenges and overcoming obstacles is the key attitude you want your child to absorb. A 'can do' approach, fostered by an affirming parent, will help a child interpret failures and grow in competence.

Sometimes, because we want our children to feel better when they don't do as well as they had wanted, we tell them the result is great when they know it isn't. Rather than doing this, we can take the opportunity to counter our children's negative way of interpreting failure. A child may say to herself, 'I'm a dumbo', or 'I can't do anything right', and that sort of self-talk will encourage passivity and giving up. As a parent you can accept your child's feelings, and perhaps tell her that when you were seven you found that task hard too, but when she is nine she will be able to do it just like her sister. All it takes is a bit of practice.

Praise is okay, and so are positive 'labels'

Praise and encouragement are as important to children as three square meals a day. Praise builds their confidence and helps them know they are loved and appreciated. Praise is powerful . . . but it can be made powerless by being used when praise isn't deserved. Be lavish in praise, be generous, but only when your daughter has done something genuinely praiseworthy.

Of course we love our children just for who they are, and we need to tell them that every day, but it's also important to learn to praise accomplishments, not just attributes. It's the difference between saying, 'What a great singer you are', and something like, 'I like the way you sing. You really put your heart and soul into it.'

Be specific about what it is you really think is praiseworthy. Rather than just general messages like 'You're okay', give her words she can use to label herself. 'Hey, that piano sounds great. You're a real musician'; 'I appreciated the way you included your little brother in that game today. A kind person like you, who helps others, is really great to have around.'

hot tip ✪

✪ Give a child praise and you will make her day.

✪ Teach her to like herself and you equip her for life.

What about overpraising?

Praise is important, but it must be appropriate. If a child is praised all the time they can become dependent on it and only function when the praise is available. Studies show that the most effective parents limit their praise. Even young children recognise constant praise as manipulative, and overpraising can make a child feel afraid and insecure. They can become unable to function without the sort of praise they have become used to. Some children feel locked in when we praise them, knowing that they are going to have to continue to produce that sort of accomplishment in order to meet with our approval.

53

Imagine — you send your daughter off to tidy her room. Some time later you look in and she obviously hasn't started to clean up, but is lying on the floor looking at her scrapbooks of ponies. If you then go in and say, 'This is marvellous, this is wonderful, you're so great at tidying up,' she's going to think, 'Mum is stupid', 'Mum is blind', and, 'Mum's praise isn't worth a thing'. You have just devalued your most potent tool.

Encouragement, however, can be a great step towards building self-esteem. So do praise the things they do, even the minor things, but when you can't praise, then encourage.

Some parents think that when they can't praise they have to criticise, but no — if you can't praise, then encourage. A better response in the situation above might be to go into the room and say, 'Hey, I see you've made a bit of a start here, I can even see a patch of floor over there, but I see some pyjamas that need to go under the pillow, some books that need to go in the bookcase, some CDs that need to go back in their cases. I'll come back in five minutes, and I know that you will do a great job.' Or, 'Morning tea will be in 10 minutes. I'll inspect then.'

You've encouraged her. You've broken the task into kid-size bites and made it more specific, and that's always a good way to get cooperation. If she gets only part of the job done right, compliment her and praise her for the bits she's done well, before reminding her of the bits that she hasn't. If she is making progress towards a goal, celebrate the steps in the right direction.

Fathers are central to their daughters' self-esteem at puberty

It seems that during puberty it is particularly significant for girls to feel valued by their dads. It's as if what he thinks about her beauty and value gives her an anchor to measure herself by, and even influences her choice of boyfriends and future partner.

Some researchers have found a stronger correlation between paternal variables such as warmth and egalitarianism (as perceived by daughters) and daughters' self-esteem than between the same maternal variables and the girls' self-esteem.

A dad sometimes expects more of his daughters, but in so doing he allows her to raise her own expectations. He will teach her about discernment, risk assessment and taking responsibility for herself. On 13 November 2007 England's *Daily Mail* quoted Robert McKenzie Johnston, the head of an independent girls' school, as saying, 'Schools should let children pick up bruises and grazed knees to help them learn how to manage danger. They should not grow up thinking "If it's allowed it must be safe", but learn to use their own judgment about what is sensible. Learning to live dangerously is a skill we are losing. In an age when girls can join the police and the army, they are at the same time surrounded by myriads of rules to keep them "safe".'

Addressing a teachers' conference, Johnston said some people used 'health and safety' as an excuse for not providing outdoor activities such as canoeing and camping. He allowed girls at his North Yorkshire school, set in four hectares of parkland, to 'toboggan down staircases and walk in the woods at night without a torch'. 'If you remove all risk you remove the soul.' We suggest fathers take an active role in this sort of 'mettle testing': it's needed nowadays.

During an interview with Nobel Prize-winning novelist Toni Morrison, she was asked why she became a great writer; what books she had read, what method she had used to structure her practice. She laughed and said, 'Oh no, that is not why I am a great writer. I am a great writer because when I was a little girl and walked into a room where my father was sitting, his eyes would light up.

'That is why I am a great writer. That is why. There is no other reason.'

— from Searching for God Knows What *by Donald Miller*

hot tip ✪

To develop a healthy self-esteem a child has to be:

- ✪ Encouraged to help in the home and be appreciated for doing so.
- ✪ Able to express her viewpoint, even when it differs from her parents'.
- ✪ Allowed to make mistakes and learn from them.
- ✪ Acknowledged as having specific talents.
- ✪ Loved and valued for who she is – not just for what she does or in comparison with anyone else.
- ✪ The subject of her parents' full attention; listened to and knowing that she has been heard.

Action lab ➳

To build a sense of value and competence in your daughter:

➳ *Cuddle up in your favourite chair and tell your daughter her own story. Start from when you went to the hospital to have her, or even earlier when you had the first scan. Tell her who saw her first, and what Grandma said when she had her first cuddle. Explain what her name means and why you chose that name for her. Tell her about her first outing, her first birthday, her christening, or her first Christmas. Tell her the three things you like best about her.*

➳ *Make sure your eyes light up when your daughter comes into the room. Every child longs for the feeling of being enjoyed and welcomed by their parents. Sadly, we often get in first with directions, corrections and complaints before we have communicated our pleasure in seeing our loved ones again. So change the order – show your delight, enjoy her company and catch up on her day, before you engage in getting the jobs done.*

➳ *Sit at the end of the bed each night and review the day. Ask her what was the nicest thing that happened, or the 'yuckiest' thing.*

➳ *Ask her, sometimes, three favourite things about her day. The favourites may be a bit bizarre and not what you expect, but they will provide an insight into what she thinks is important.*

➳ *Reinterpret negative personal situations for her.*

➤➤ *Consciously use loving words: 'All your practising has paid off. I can hardly believe what I heard'; 'It's fun to be with you. You brighten my life'; 'Turn around and let Dad see this.' Use phrases that build self-esteem: 'You can be proud of yourself because . . .'; 'I really appreciated seeing you . . .'; 'I'm impressed!'*

➤➤ *Encourage achievement and an entrepreneurial spirit. Use big words.*

➤➤ *When she reaches eight or nine years old, buy her a book such as Sylvia Rimm's See Jane Win: A Smart Girl's Guide to Success.*

➤➤ *As a family create a culture of celebration. Award weekly accolades. This could be your family's version of an 'award' ceremony. It is a way of offering acknowledgement to family members, and having others in the family cheer and clap for them.*

➤➤ *Award vouchers or a chocolate fish for jobs well done, an unnoticed kindness, good marks at school, a win at a sport or a small achievement such as finishing a school project. Have someone produce a virtual drum-roll or trumpet accolade before each announcement.*

➤➤ *Allow one person to eat off a special red plate when they have done something praiseworthy — learned to tie their shoe laces, done well in a test, passed their driver's licence (see page 87).*

in summary

HOW TO BUILD SELF-ESTEEM

To develop their daughter's self-esteem parents need to:

- Understand something about her nature, and parent her in a way that makes her feel accepted.
- Encourage her — give her lots of the right sort of attention, approval from her family and friends, and the sense that she can be proud of her own achievements and character.
- Help her to keep alive her dreams for her life.
- Encourage her to participate in sport — it will help her develop skills and confidence, and create another community of friends.
- Encourage her creativity, which will contribute to a sense of significance.
- Nurture feelings of connectedness and belonging.
- Offer regular, but appropriate praise. Your warm appreciation and timely 'Well done' matters — it will lead your daughter into knowing how to praise herself, because she knows the praise is deserved.

Chapter 5

Girls and their culture

Those of us raising girls, especially prepubescent girls, who are already under great internal stress, should pay particular attention to our culture's general social over-stimulation and hyper-stress today. More and more early adolescent girls are over stimulated by social technologies than they were a hundred years ago. Simultaneously, they experience this increased stress without compensatory family and extended family safety.

— **Michael Gurian,** The Wonder of Girls

Children are now targeted not only through TV ads, but via internet pop-ups and e-mail as well as through product placements in programmes and on websites. The electronic media allow plenty of opportunities for the two great learning devices: imitation and repetition.

— **Sue Palmer,** Detoxing Childhood

We had a revolution, and now girls can do anything they want to, though it's turning out not to be that simple. The empire struck back, and ugly forces of commercial greed rushed into the vacuum created by the collapse of the old values, and created for girls a whole new slavery; you have to be slender. You have to have big breasts, even if it means slicing your chest open and sliding in slabs of silicone. You have to work your whole life long, even if you simply long for some peace and quiet with your new baby, or to be creative, or have some time to just be. You have to have it all.

— **Gisela Preuschoff,** Raising Girls

Although there are many positives for girls in today's culture, alongside those positives are numerous other influences that subtly, and not so subtly, work to undermine their confidence. Yes, girls can do just about anything that their male counterparts can do, and some would say that it is a girls' world. Yet the fascinating fact is that in the post-feminist era girls are suffering the most from a revolution that has not necessarily protected their feminine 'nature' and seems obsessed with image, acquisition and achievement, sometimes at the cost of those things that make us human — time to think, play and enjoy relationships.

As we have pointed out, girls' natural desire for intimacy is rooted deep in their biology and psychology. Whereas the testosterone needed to operate in a competitive work environment energises men, it depletes women. And the individualism and materialism at the core of modern society tend to work against the female need for connection. Through the media, marketers have an entry into our lives to peddle material goods, playing on human frailty and our insecurities to get us hooked. To be thin and sexually attractive is to be esteemed in popular culture, as is to be rich or 'cool', whatever that means. Such artificial measurements of worth offer false bearings for a girl looking for a compass to see her through to womanhood.

Girls are acutely sensitive to their culture and can be distressed to be out of step with it. It could be said that one of a girl's worst fears is to be left out and alone.

Our modern culture is particularly toxic to girls in that it is so appearance driven. Look at any magazine for girls or women and you will find quizzes relating to appearance, relationships or diets, all of which are basically saying 'Do you measure up? Are you good enough?' It is cruel for girls to be tested in such shallow ways, playing upon their fears about their acceptance within the culture.

The challenges for parents

Traditionally parents and older women introduced their daughters to the current culture. Now, unfortunately, parents need to protect their girls from many aspects of the culture. In other words, we need to equip them to be culturally smart. We need to be proactive and set a different agenda in our homes, to challenge and where necessary override messages driven home by the media.

This is not to say that we shouldn't enable our daughters to grow in the sort of individuality, poise and grace that allows them to radiate their own special beauty. They can certainly learn to dress creatively and use clothes and fabric with flair and confidence. But we need to affirm those things for different reasons than the materialism fuelled by the shallow motive of greed.

We need to value qualities other than outward appearance, teaching our daughters to be comfortable in her own skin. If we see their beauty in who they are and in their own individual attractiveness, including their character and their energy, then we are well on the way to growing girls who will not be squeezed into a false mould of 'image-driven' culture. In the words of one young woman who had never had the genes to be stick-thin, even as a young teenager, 'When I was about 12 or 13 . . . you know, when you are really insecure about yourself, all over the place with your moods and starting to get the odd pimple . . . if I ever dressed up to go somewhere, my dad would "pretend" that he was just blown away by how I looked. [The dad assures us that there was no pretending.] . . . Now when I look back, I realise how important that was in getting me through that awkward time. His view of me really helped me view myself a lot more positively.'

From their daughter's earliest days parents need to foil the society-driven imperative to be thin, beautiful and sexually available. What you value will be absorbed by your daughter. As you value the quality of her inner person, and value not appearances but 'inner beauty' in others, she will learn to look for those qualities in herself and her friends and will be less likely to define herself by her body.

While it is important and valid to model healthy living — looking after ourselves, valuing grooming and fitness — mirrors can be deceptive, leaving us feeling dissatisfied and chasing after the 'idol' of how we should look.

Mothers, be especially conscious of your comments during this time; even throw-away remarks can be interpreted by your daughter as reflecting her inadequacies. Raising a daughter is a big responsibility, and sometimes we parents might need to take an inventory of our own self-talk. Is it too negative? How do we view ourselves? If, as a mother, you are constantly obsessed with your weight or what you have, or wear, you will pass on those subliminal messages to your daughter. She loves you and wants to be like you.

When your daughter has a friend over, show that you value the qualities of her character. Affirm the qualities in her friends that your daughter can replicate, not superficial or external ones. For instance, if you say, 'We loved having Katie over to play . . . Wow, hasn't she got beautiful blonde curls!' there is nothing your young daughter, a straight-haired brunette, can do about that until the day she can get her hands on a bottle of hair colouring. But if you affirm qualities in Katie, like the fact that she was so helpful or polite, or gracious in the way she asked for things, you will show your daughter that those are the things that really matter.

Provide a model by having a wide range of friends yourself whom you value for who they are — their vibrancy, their love of life, their interests and creativity — not for what they look like, how much they weigh or what they wear.

> We can help girls develop a broader appreciation of beauty by surrounding them with a richness of art, music, nature, people and cultural experiences.
>
> — **Sally Shanks,** *counsellor*

Popular culture

The number of social commentators and psychologists who are becoming concerned about the influence of popular culture on girls is increasing noticeably, to the extent that what was formerly a trickle has now become an avalanche. We are now being told that there is the equivalent of an epidemic of eating disorders among girls in the Western world.

Using peer-reviewed research, the Australian Women's Forum recently created a TV documentary, *Faking It*, for parents. The forum found documented evidence of our culture's negative effects on young girls that cannot be dismissed. A variety of malaises were linked to the whole culture of thinness and early sexualisation promoted by magazines and the fashion industry. The forum found that the increase in eating disorders, self-harming, low self-image, academic failure and depression in young girls could be strongly linked to unrealistic images and diet fads promoted in what are considered mainstream magazines. It quoted *Girlfriend, Marie Claire, Cosmopolitan* and *Dolly*, and found their contribution to this epidemic to be of great concern: 'Girls are not using their true talents, but worrying about whether they are "hot", skinny, or have the right bra size.'

In the documentary, girls and young women aged between six and 24 talked about the way they are influenced by magazines, the media and 'celebrities'. The film revealed a disturbing level of dissatisfaction with their appearance felt by even the youngest girls. As they flicked through fashion and beauty magazines, primary-school girls said the magazines made them want to be skinny and go on diets. Most girls, the documentary-makers said, think they are too fat when in fact they are not, and 10- and 11-year-olds are asking their teachers what diets they are on.

At the same time, bikini model Brooke, 24, described how airbrushing and digital enhancement mean she does not even recognise herself in the magazines she poses for. The models in the airbrushed photographs are not even real, so these girls are in fact trying to live up to something that doesn't actually exist.

You are not just your body.

— **Dave Riddell,** *counsellor*

Living in the culture but choosing what you will value

Concentric circles of connection

Your daughter's strong relationships will give her a sense of significance. Strong family connections, good relationships with her wider family, and links with the community through clubs, sport or youth groups will provide the concentric circles of connection and belonging she needs.

They will provide her with 'bearings' on her value and worth as a person, and a sense of place and purpose in the world: a reality check on what matters. These relationships will also provide a circle group of other adults who care about her, who have a positive input into her life, and on whom she can rely when tough situations arise.

The influence of marketers

The influence of marketers on our children cannot be overestimated. They have a huge impact on what clothes and accessories girls want to wear, what bands they want to listen to, and what events they want to attend. Parents should find the 'slut culture' demeaning. The irony of promoting provocative clothing for young children in a sexualised culture must not be missed by parents. It is our job to offer them a protected childhood, a time of innocence and safety, where they can relax, mature in an appropriate way, and become the person they were born to be.

In her book *Detoxing Childhood*, Sue Palmer catalogues some of the inappropriate toys marketed to young girls: a 'Secret Date' collection of dolls for six-year-olds, complete with two champagne glasses; sexy underwear for little girls, and kids' gear that includes fully equipped hairdressing salons and mini-briefcases. She explains how they are all part of 'KAGOY', a marketing strategy based on the premise 'Kids Are Growing Older Younger'. Sue Palmer observes, 'I always wonder whether the mothers who buy sexy clothing for their pre-teenage daughters and let them go out plastered in make-up are the same mothers who protest stridently about paedophiles . . . and whether they ever make the rather obvious connection.'

It's important that parents don't become super-police and create a 'No' culture, but rather are aware of the situation and sensitively guide it back to balance. I loved the action of the smart mother who emailed me recently to tell me about an interchange she had had with her daughter in a swimsuit boutique. The family were planning a holiday in Fiji and her 13-year-old daughter needed a new swimsuit. The shop assistant kept guiding her towards the skimpiest bikinis one could imagine. The mother felt her daughter didn't need this type of exposure in the holiday resort, and tried to guide her towards a more sensible bikini choice for her age. Oblivious to her manoeuvres, the assistant kept heading the girl back to the skimpy-bikini rack. Just as she was becoming desperate, the mother remembered hearing me talk about the importance of using humour in challenging parenting situations. So with a smile she said to her daughter, 'Why don't I buy one of those too and we will be twinnies!' Guess what — the skimpy bikini didn't get bought.

Child sexualisation is no game

The sexualisation of children stems from the fact that many of the corporations that create and sell popular culture and fashions to teenage girls and adult women are now competing to capture girl-children's allegiance to their brands. In doing so, they aim to build both an immediate and a future market for their products. But premature sexualisation has risks for children. One such risk is an unhealthy focus on body image and appearance, leading sometimes to eating disorders.

While some dismiss these concerns with the observation that little girls have tottered around in their mother's high-heels since the year dot, this is not the nature of these concerns. Moving children away from more traditional and developmentally appropriate games and activities, and focusing instead on body image and appearance, has brought with it an avalanche of eating disorders among even young children.

As the producers of *Faking It* discovered, studies show that girls as young as six and seven are now concerned about their physical appearance, particularly their weight, and that even at this early age some are beginning to develop 'disordered eating behaviours'. This concern with weight is clearly not related to childhood obesity. In one study of girls aged between nine and 12, half wanted to be thinner, but only 15 per cent were in any way overweight according to medical criteria.

There is also some evidence that children are developing severe eating disorders — usually anorexia — at earlier ages. Eating disorders are difficult to treat, and they can be fatal. Medical experts and psychologists are extremely concerned and this apparent trend is now being carefully monitored.

Fathers have a powerful opportunity to reject the 'culture of appearance'

An interesting observation from a 1996 study of the dieting beliefs and behaviours of 13- and 14-year-old girls, published that year in the *Journal of Adolescent Health*, was that the *fathers'* dieting behaviour and their encouragement to diet were associated with a range of behaviours in their daughters — including crash dieting, purging and vomiting.

More recently, in 2003, the University of Auckland study 'Exploring paternal influences on the dieting behaviours of adolescent girls' also showed that fathers played an influential role in determining the dieting behaviour of their adolescent daughters. Girls whose fathers placed a high importance on weight control and physical attractiveness were significantly more likely to report having vomited to lose weight — 100 per cent of the fathers of these girls perceived their daughters to be larger than ideal.

The authors concluded that a father's strong belief in the importance of attractiveness and diet control, along with a perception that their daughter is larger than ideal, appears to be a particularly potent combination in regard to his daughter's body satisfaction and attitude towards weight loss.

It seems that having a great relationship with her father is of huge importance for a girl. His affirming, loving hugging, and his encouragement of her for who she is — loving every aspect of her just the way she is — are the best antidotes to her potential obsession with weight and diet. For more on this see chapter 13, 'Dads and daughters'.

Another risk of premature sexualisation is that it may encourage sexual predation on children.

Yes, those who sexually abuse children are wholly responsible for their abhorrent actions. But there is a risk that publicly displaying sexualised images of children undermines the existing social prohibition against seeing children as sexually interesting.

As the makers of *Faking It* put it, 'G-string swimsuits being marketed for two-year-olds; peek-a-boo pole-dancing kits for small girls who are encouraged to earn money for dancing sexually for their family; the Bratz doll babies: the manufacturers say these babies know how to flaunt it — what are little girls, even babies, flaunting?'

We must recognise this culture for what it is and fight to protect our daughters from it.

Not just 'safe' – teach her about real love

Unfortunately, sometimes the only thing a girl hears about in relation to her sexual behaviour is the concept of being 'safe'. One of the great challenges of parenting today is to reconnect sex with love, intimacy and faithfulness. Contrary to the representations on today's celluloid and digital media, shallow, transient relationships are not the source of happiness for most women. The female nature in particular has a deep need for intimacy and commitment. Current society is strewn with sad stories of women who have settled for casual sex and one-night stands, only to find themselves walked over or abandoned. Yes, this generation of girls has the opportunity to make well-informed choices about potential boyfriends or partners, but in practice that is not what is happening. We are a generation raising our girls on feelings, and unfortunately feelings can lie. Gossip magazines can portray an idealised version of serial relationships with the opposite sex, but they can't convey the personal pain of broken relationships and rejection that affect women so deeply. One only has to observe the tragedy of the unravelling lives of such teenage icons as Britney Spears and Paris Hilton to realise that if fame and beauty are one's only goals, they are illusory crowns and false comforters.

hot tip ✪

What a girl needs most when she is growing up is the security that she is not only Okay but also extremely valuable and precious, and she really needs her parents' protection from the invasive culture of 'appearance'. Many girls and women have a soundtrack constantly running in their heads, about whether they are measuring up or not, and this is why our encouragement matters so much.

Value your daughter highly and she will value herself. As parents we have a major role in helping our daughters to enjoy a wide variety of safe friendships, showing them how to establish and maintain personal boundaries, and teaching them to recognise and value character in potential boyfriends, spouses and soulmates.

We can create a climate within our own friendships and social groups that will offer our daughters the possibility of a rich social life and healthy male friendships. Ideally we can show through our own relationships what real love is, the beauty of being faithful, and how she can set truly worthy goals for her future.

Protecting childhood

So how do you help your daughter hold onto her childlike, playful self for as long as possible?

The challenge for parents is to provide safe havens from the toxic side of our culture. Create family events that give your daughter 'time out' from the culture. Camping holidays, visits to Grandma, playing with younger cousins, family traditions and celebrations and journalling will all provide your daughter with safe havens of childhood. Keep birthday parties simple, with the emphasis on friendship and creativity. Try to avoid buying into highly sophisticated events that push girls towards adult activities that are inappropriate for their age group.

Take charge of her media diet from the start. If you begin with half an hour of screen time for preschoolers, then designated nights for computer time for five- and six-year olds, she will learn that the computer has a place in her life, but not a dominating one. There are some homes in which the television never goes off, and researchers are now blaming even background television for the rise of attention-deficit disorders. Your daughter needs times of peace and space, creative play and quiet reading. Take charge of the atmosphere in your own home. Speak up about tacky, explicit billboards and magazine posters in your community.

'MEDIA-PROOF YOUR KIDS OR KAGOY WILL GET THEM'

This was a headline in The Times *on 11 August 2007. The article underneath read:*

Marketers zero in on kids to exploit the guilt of parents not spending enough time with their kids; to capitalise on pester-power; and to build brand loyalty from the earliest years. Their message, 'You are what you own.'

Did you know: Companies use kids as street scouts and pay them to report on trends and promote brands. Wal-Mart's website showed kids how to email their parents an 'I want' Christmas list. An ad agency used teeny-bopper concerts to 'seed' promo figures, which also featured on websites visited by kids and on gifts of clothing to TV presenters.

The difference for this generation

Women have tended to care about values and, as nurturers, see the future through their children. As a result they were often the ones who fought for social causes and a better future, often using their female intuition and ability to network as forces for good.

In previous generations women and girls were encouraged to work on their *character*. Now girls are insidiously programmed to work on their *appearance*. Think about the literature of a generation or two ago. Jane Austen and Louisa May Alcott provided a very different media diet than *Sex in the City* and *Shortland Street*, in which feelings rather than character and morality drive decisions. The media, by its very nature, loves to fascinate through sensation. Unfortunately, without 'earthed' and mature adults to interpret and challenge the stories and impressions that emanate from television and magazines, girls' romantic natures lead them to absorb these pseudo truths. While your daughter is pondering the meaning of life she needs moral boundaries and rules. And the media couldn't care less.

Technology

If your daughter wishes, she can 'text' you out of her life. Your challenge is to build trust and use technology to enhance your lives, not oppress them.

Mobile phones have become the new route to acceptance, and they can be used to bully and intimidate girls far more easily than their male counterparts. Because girls are so relational they will take personally the content of text messages, and replay them over and over. If they are sent a bullying text they will wonder what it is about them that would make someone send something so awful. More often than not a boy will just delete a demeaning message, and think 'What an idiot', but a girl will let it play like a record in her head, trying to find the reason behind it.

Mobiles need to be set up from the start with an eye to protecting your daughter. We suggest that initially she has the use of a family cellphone, which enables parents to check messages and texts regularly, and help her deal with any damaging ones. When she does get her own mobile, have her set up a business plan so she knows how she will pay for and manage it, and what rules she will set for herself about her conduct.

Establish a culture in your family in which television, phones, computers, games, etc. are privileges, not rights, and where you retain the right to control your children's access to them. You can tell older children that, 'The internet and phone are privileges — privileges come from trust, and trust comes from transparency. Therefore I retain the right to review your internet and phone histories' (i.e. review what sites they have visited and what their text chats have been about).

TEXT ETIQUETTE FOR TEENAGERS

❖ *Turn your phone off during movies, meals and at bedtime.*

❖ *Don't feel you have to respond to texts instantly. Keep your own boundaries. Similarly, don't text-nag someone for a reply.*

❖ *It is rude to text or read texts while someone is trying to interact with you. To be present physically but absent emotionally is very insulting.*

❖ *Some things are always going to be better face-to-face. 'Luv u' and 'Miss u' are fine, but breaking up by text ('C u l8r — not') is harsh and cowardly.*

What are the ground rules around media and technology?

First of all, no media should be dodgy or dangerous — more of that later. Secondly, technology should make up only a small part of a balanced lifestyle, mixed in with plenty of active play, reading, chores, rest, etc. Thirdly, let your daughter know that there are priorities in your family. Mealtimes, for instance, have a high priority and are a media-free zone: the TV is turned off, the computer is shut down, and there is no texting at the table. Homework, chores and face-to face contact with visitors all rate as a priority.

The 'Grandma's Rule' formula ('You can do what you want to do when you've done what you have to do') works well here:

'Yes, you can go on the computer, after you've got that homework finished.'

'I'll put that video on after your bath.'

'You can use the computer, but not until after tea. There are a few things I want you to do first.'

Be wary of early media overload

Occasionally popping your preschooler in front of the 'cyber-sitter' to watch a DVD of *My Little Pony* won't ruin her. But it won't teach her to talk and think either. Perhaps the most insidious thing about electronic media is that these waste precious time at the crucial stages of children's lives when they need to interact with others, especially parents. Face-to-face human contact, playing, talking, singing and dancing are the proven ways to develop healthy brains and bodies.

hot tip ✪

- ✪ Switch off all mobiles; including Mum and Dad's, at mealtimes and after 8pm. Have everyone put them in a basket in the kitchen.
- ✪ If your daughter wants a mobile get her to write up a business plan setting out how she will pay for it, and then some rules around how she will use it.

Protect your daughter from cyber-nasties

Letting your children wander the internet without guidance or protection is very risky.

- Social pages like Bebo and MySpace (along with texting) are the new way spineless bullies can make other kids miserable.
- Many children unwisely arrange 'real-world' meetings with people they meet online.
- Girls have been known to use their parents' credit cards to run up bills on virtual wardrobes and even virtual real estate.

Action lab ➥

Some limits to put around your kids' internet behaviour:

➥ *Have the computer in a public part of the house where it can be monitored. If you have other computers at home, disable or password-protect internet access. No TVs or computers in bedrooms.*

➥ *Use filtering software or a filtered internet provider.*

➤➤ Limit the sites children are allowed to visit: if they want to go elsewhere, you have to be there. Set up access to the sites they are allowed through the 'Favourites' icon.

➤➤ Read the safety information on Bebo and MySpace (every page has safety, blocking and privacy links) and make sure your children understand that they can and should block and report rude or abusive behaviour.

➤➤ Set their page up so it is only accessible to people they know. Get them to take you through their address book — do they really know who these people are? Remind them that all these people can read what is written on their page.

➤➤ Sign on and get your own Bebo and MySpace membership — you can find out a lot about your daughter's world by reading her page and her friends' pages.

➤➤ As a family, establish TV and computer rules for your young children. Then remind them: 'Remember the family rule!'

➤➤ Talk with other families who share your values, and create a sense that these are everyone's rules; for example, half an hour of screentime, or half an hour twice a week.

➤➤ School-age children can take part in the process of writing up your family rules for the computer and television.

The wrong world

Our children should live in *our* world, not the world created by media cyber-gods. Children are amazingly pliable and easily shaped by influences early in life. During their years of innocence and vulnerability, nothing should get to them that you don't approve of. If you take seriously your privilege of teaching them the values and wisdom that they will take into later life, you need to be careful of anything that contradicts or dilutes your messages.

The media shows your daughter a world with values that may be very different from your own. Even very young children get to see that in media-land it is the pretty and attractive people who have the friends and success. All sorts of values around materialism and sexuality get peddled, not only in stories and lyrics, but also in the ads. Some of the values are toxic, some are just plain useless: one study of small children showed that they learnt from cartoons that bad people always talk funny. The bad guys on their shows always had strange, stilted 'villain' accents. What a useful thing to learn!

DVDs and television

Sometimes the content and images on TV, and in CDs and DVDs are downright objectionable. If a person came into your home and started talking or acting like that in front of your children you'd kick them out pretty quickly, so don't tolerate it from the uninvited guests on your television.

Show respect for women and girls in front of family members

Use your own heart as the standard in your home. Don't be embarrassed that your tastes and ideas of decency conflict with the morals of some TV producer. Imagine this scenario: you walk into the room and your kids are watching a music video, and there is just too much flesh — too much seems to be moving on the screen at once. Say, 'As a woman, that offends me: turn it off or watch something else, please.' If they reply, 'It's not too rude!' you could ask, 'Well, what *would* be too rude?' They will think about it, not want to get into *that* argument, and go and change the channel. A male colleague says that as a dad he uses the words, 'I am trying to respect women and that doesn't make it easy — turn it off.'

As you interact with their viewing, they will soon get an idea of what your standards are, especially if you model discernment yourself. If they see you monitoring and turning off your own programmes, and not just theirs, the message will be clear and consistent.

What about someone else's house?

In his book *The Wonder of Girls*, Michael Gurian tells how his eight-year-old daughter had watched *The Matrix* during a sleepover at her girlfriend's house. This was the second time his daughter had seen a movie at this friend's house that as a psychologist and caring father he considered 'dangerous to her brain's developmental age'. (The first had been the violent *The Mummy*.) He realised it was time to decide whether his daughter could go to that house again.

He contacted the other family, who couldn't promise that what was being watched by the older children in the household wouldn't be watched by the younger ones too. Although his daughter protested that she loved going to her friend's house, from then on the friend came to their house for overnighters, not the other way around. He records that he felt like an ogre making this rule, but he knew the decision was right for his daughter's age and stage of development. In Michael Gurian's words: 'The world of stories (media, books, movies, MTV) is a world in which our children wander relatively aimlessly. Until our children have completed the lion's share of their brain's emotional and moral development (by about 16), we cannot be too vigilant about what stories we find "worthy" for them. When they are seven and eight, their brains cannot abstract well enough to integrate the violence of *The Matrix* into the compelling moral scheme of the movie. Thus, the movie does their development — at that age — more harm than good. At that age, books and movies need to be "harmlessly imaginative", without demeaning sex, violence, or immoral messages, and they must have uncomplicated moral conclusions.'

Isolated within a family

Modern technology can unite people on different sides of the planet, yet can separate people in the same room. One of the interesting features of modern media is that it can push families apart as each person pursues their own form of entertainment. When our generation was introduced to television back in the one-channel black-and-white 1960s, the whole family watched it together.

Now children and teens have their own programmes, even their own channels, which they frequently watch on their own sets. A family can all be together in the lounge, but one might be on the computer, another listening to music on her iPod, and others on PlayStation.

Create an alternative culture

Everyone wants to feel like they are part of a team and that they matter in that team. Your family can become the team that your daughter most wants to be part of.

The most recent research about preventing teenagers developing dysfunctional behaviour reveals an enlightening fact: what stops them behaving badly is the thought of letting their parents and their family down. Providing a home in which your daughter can unload, be appreciated and have fun is the best way to protect her from shallow values. It starts with fun and communication. The trust you build and the love you show over many years put in place cords of connectedness that will be stronger than any external pressures.

Have daily doses of fun, and build traditions that make your family special. One father of three girls says he takes his girls on a yearly expedition. It is just a long weekend, which they plan together. Each girl has a certain amount of time during which she is in charge of what they do. For example, they may go on a train trip to another city, and each girl will choose an activity or an attraction to visit. She must research the attraction, plan how they will get there, and stay within a budget.

Make mealtimes a place where everyone contributes, debates, asks questions and tells stories. If you don't come from a family that used the meal table as a place of conversation and connection, then set it up in this generation. Read to your children at the dinner table, and ask them questions about the story.

Try some of these conversation starters:

- What is one thing you couldn't live without?
- Describe your perfect day.
- What job would you never want to have?
- What is your favourite room in our house? Why?
- Who is someone you look up to?

Children love to know that you are interested in what they think.

Just think for a moment of the value of the meal table. If it is expected that everyone will be there, unless excused for a specific reason, then you have a way of touching base each day and being involved with your children. The rule of checking in for the meal means teenagers can't drift into their own world of 'grunts' and eating out of the fridge. The mealtime chatter lets you find out about what is going on in their lives and let you add your perspective to the mix.

If children are allowed to pick at food, decide when they want to eat, or help themselves from the fridge and sit in front of the TV, then you have lost a simple battle of compliance and connection. If your children know that they must come to the table when called, perhaps not begin eating until grace has been said, and phone in if for any reason they will not be at dinner, then the family will function well. The meal table is the centrepiece of communication. Meal time provides the opportunity to hand on generational wisdom, to debrief and dust your children down if they have had a hard day.

hot tip ✪

MONITOR AND TAKE CHARGE OF MEDIA CULTURE IN YOUR HOME

✪ Let older children earn media tokens by playing outside for an amount of time. Credit every hour of outside play time with half an hour of media time.

✪ Turn the content of what your daughter watches into a discussion at the meal table or bedtime. Ask her to recall and explain the plot, then talk about the characters and the decisions they made. Encourage her to be 'critical', questioning a story rather than just swallowing it whole.

✪ Have half an hour of reading every day – make it a family rule. Begin by reading to your daughter, then let her read to you.

✪ Budget your daughter's media consumption by setting a limited number of hours she can watch TV each week. Help her to plan how she will spend those media hours. This will train her to be more discerning, rather than just passively soaking up whatever is fired at her. It also keeps you in the loop as to what she is watching.

✪ Since it's not going to happen by accident, it will have to happen on purpose: engineer times together. Chose a DVD you can all watch, or better still, switch off the electronics and play a board game.

○   Stay in touch. Children need a catalyst to get them talking. Use questions that offer your daughter an opportunity to tell you more about herself.

○   Have a movie night. Let your daughter make tickets, organise the popcorn and treats, or invite a special friend over. Half the fun is in the preparation. Make sure the movie is selected under your supervision, from the 'G' or 'PG' section of the video store.

○   Crazy memories are great memories. Take what is ordinary and 'everydayish' and add a new slant to it. Add a bit of the unexpected to meals by changing the time, place, utensils and décor. Serve the meal backwards, have a hide-and-seek meal (where the children must follow clues to find each course), or have a picnic in front of the fire.

○   Press 'Play'. Running around after your kids isn't the same as running around with your kids. Don't forget to occasionally press 'Pause' and then 'Play' and just spend some time playing with your daughter. Get down on the floor and make huts out of blankets, have a tea party and see if you can find that board game to play after dinner.

○   Model activity yourself. Draw your daughter into hobbies, sport and active pastimes. Have TV-free nights and a curfew on mobiles after 8pm.

in summary ✏

HOW PARENTS CAN PROTECT THEIR DAUGHTERS FROM THE TOXICITY OF THE CURRENT CULTURE

Girls need parents who:

- Set a different agenda in their homes to challenge the messages driven home by the media.
- See their daughter's beauty in who she is, not what she looks like.
- Provide a model by having a wide range of friends who are valued for who they are, not for what they look like, how much they weigh or what they wear.
- Are careful not to pass on subliminal messages about weight loss by being overconcerned with their own, and their daughter's, appearance. Daughters pick up messages from their mother's behaviour, but are also very responsive to their fathers' perceptions and opinions.
- Teach them about real love – not just 'safe' sexual behaviour.
- Show them how to establish and maintain personal boundaries.
- Provide a safe haven and family times that provide time out from the culture.
- Use technology wisely and set up ground rules.
- Show respect for all women and girls.

Chapter 6

A family in which your daughter will thrive

Psychiatry must be concerned with two basic psychological needs; the need to love and be loved and the need to feel that we are worthwhile to ourselves and to others.

— **William Glasser,** *father of reality therapy*

When a child comes into your life you must take care to give it family, however you define it, and history and community. For the child learns of life from its context. You must offer your highest vision of good, and a sense of moral purpose, and a healthy vision of the world outside. Above all you must be prepared to give your child time. Because time shapes with silent hands.

— **Kent Nerburn,** Simple Truths

Every day when my dad came home from his long, hard days working as a butcher, Mum, my sister and I would drop whatever we were doing and meet him in the kitchen for a big hug and discussion about our respective days . . . We'd stand there hugging and chatting for ages, content in a sliver of time.

— **Helen Medlyn,** *mezzo-soprano*

Childhood is over so quickly. Your girls won't remember the tidy pot-cupboard or the expensive curtains — but they will remember the spontaneous picnics, the hide-and-seek dinners, and the delight on your face when they present you with a freshly picked bunch of daisies. A child reflects love, and we are responsible for showing them what unconditional acceptance, welcome and belonging look like. Give your girls the sense that they are valued members of the family 'team'. Remember, when a child joins a family, that family should already stand for something.

> Remember, when a child joins a family, that family should already stand for something.

To a girl, no conversation equals no interest

Many people these days treat parenting as a management task. By the time their first child is born they often have an established career, and so the baby is born into a busy lifestyle.

Unfortunately children can't be treated like a series of 'to do' lists, and parenting isn't something that can just be fitted in around other things. Girls especially need lots of conversation and connection.

Growing great girls is a task that will impact on the next generation and many more generations to come. If your daughter is nurtured and celebrated, laughed with, and given skills and an ethic to live by she will become a contributor, not just a taker. In turn she will hand on the building blocks of a meaningful life to her own children.

So what does a healthy family look like?

Actually, experts tell us that happy children tend to come from families in which the parents have full, happy lives themselves. Couples who have passions, friends and hobbies, and make time to help others, give their children a priceless foundation for life.

Just loving your daughter as the centre of the universe, without building a meaningful life around her, doesn't give her a picture of what a satisfying life looks like. Adults who are positive and optimistic tend to communicate their joy of life to their children. By enabling your daughter to watch your reactions, in joy and in pain, and to see how you make your life fulfilling in both good times and bad, you are being the best teacher and offering the best gift you can to your daughter.

The power of 'WE' and the three-legged stool of parenting

Parenting, it always seems to us, is like a three-legged stool. For a three-legged stool to be effective each leg must be the same length, or in parenting, of equal importance.

The first leg in parenting is fun and communication. The second leg is monitoring systems (boundaries and discipline) and the third is teaching character and virtues. If we parent with only one or even two of these legs we may gain cooperation, as with mice in a laboratory, but we are unlikely to win our daughter's heart and give her the strength to use her voice and skills to take charge of her own life.

The first leg of the stool — fun and communication

A family needs lots of fun and love. Games and laughter, doing things together, picnics, rituals and celebrations are the living glue that connects a family. These are the things that make us feel significant and part of something bigger, and they will give your daughter that community that her nature longs for.

Even the family chores can be turned into something fun if you begin at the right age. Use the power of the phrase, 'In our family we . . .'. For example, 'In our family, when you are two you are allowed to make your own bed.' At two your daughter can pull up the duvet on her own. Or, 'In our family when you are three you are allowed to unpack the dishwasher, and at four set the table.' At five she will discover that these are really jobs, but already she is hooked!

To tell a small daughter to go and clean her room is too much, but if you put on her favourite CD and say 'Let's see if we can get this room cleaned before the Barney song finishes', she will see it as a community project. In our family I quickly discovered that a daughter thinks you are as talented as any Hollywood actor. Unfortunately this view changes by the time she is 11 or 12, so take advantage of this window!

I used to play a number of Hollywood characters. In those days my favourite was Colonel Klink from the television comedy *Hogan's Heroes*. I would say to my children in a German accent, 'I'm tired of these filthy cells! I'm insisting zat you clean up your cells and reach to zee highest perfection!' Then I would goof around and goose-step up and down. I would then get them to stand outside their bedroom doors as I inspected their 'cells'. I would poke around and comment on their rooms, then I would say something like, 'I vont to tell you, you have at last reached my very high standards and for zat reason I want to give you your ultimate German reward . . . a change of undervear! Andrew will change with Kim, Kim will change with Jonathan, and Jonathan will change with Andrew.' That may not be a very original joke, but I was amazed at how often the children would say, 'Dad, would you do the Colonel Klink joke again!'

Having started early, cleaning rooms became a family affair and it wasn't such a huge deal when we called for a clean-up and inspection. Sometimes successfully completed jobs were celebrated with a virtual trumpet fanfare, and then accolades of a chocolate fish or a special morning tea! The key is that they learn that the job has a beginning, an end and a celebration to follow. You are growing a family that learns they are part of something bigger, that they can enjoy the feeling of teamwork, and of finishing a task then patting themselves on the back for a job well done.

When your daughter is little, stage 'after dinner games' or 'after bath games' such as races, or being pulled on a rug around the house. Join together in dancing and action songs such as the 'hokey tokey' or the elephant song, where she rides on your back and then gets thrown onto the couch. Let your daughter squeal with delight at being thrown high or tickled by the tickling monster.

With your older daughters, play favourite CDs and boogie while doing the dishes together.

Have family nights and let your children take turns at being leader for the week and planning the activity. You may have a back-to-front meal, a meal by candlelight, or one where you throw a dice and the courses come out in the order of the throw. Friday-night DVDs, 'pizza and Pictionary', fruit cake, flags, ice-cream on top of the cornflakes — these are all the building blocks of a home that has a sense of team and belonging.

hot tip ✪

✪ Let your daughter enjoy being the centre of attention on her birthday. Make a birthday crown for your young daughter and, as we've mentioned before, each year have the rest of the family create a banner for her. It can be made out of newsprint, but has as its theme whatever she is into at the time (like fashion or sport). When she comes out in the morning her banner is hanging up in the family room to greet her.

Make mealtimes a highlight

One of the general memories most of us have of growing up is mealtimes. Some people remember them as fun, convivial and full of conversation; others remember being told to 'Just eat up', and don't remember ever being talked to or asked for a contribution.

A plethora of research shows that eating together as a family is one of the best predictors of children achieving well at school, as well as protection against their becoming involved with drugs and alcohol abuse in the future. Children need to eat, and whether the day has been good, bad or a real 'meltdown', there is something important about being together, catching up on the day and regrouping as a unit. It nurtures a sense of belonging in children; they belong somewhere to someone — this is my tribe; I'm a member of this team.

The feeling of connection and the warm atmosphere created in your home can have great repercussions. You may feel exhausted at the end of the day and just want to feed the children with as little fuss as possible, but even a little effort will be amply rewarded through your children's cooperation and memories. Our daughter has vivid memories of fondues and treasure-hunt dinners when she was little. We may only have done each of them three or four times, but ask her what her best childhood memories are and she'll tell you every time it was those magical dinners.

The custom of gathering together as a family for a meal each night seems to be dying away, at a time when the world our children must negotiate is becoming more and more impersonal as a result of technology and 'busyness'. Jane Nelsen, a family therapist and author of the book *Positive Discipline*, says children need happy family times together: 'Self-esteem comes from having a sense of belonging and knowing that our contributions are heard and worthwhile.' Read to your children at the dinner table and run quizzes about what you have read, reinforcing that you want to know what they think.

Remember, any alternative to the norm is fun for children, so creating memorable mealtimes doesn't have to be complicated. Write your special dinner on the family noticeboard and let everyone look forward to it all week — it might have a movie-night theme, be a fondue Friday, or a 'What do you think?' night, which may bring up all sorts of interesting revelations for parents!

Our daughter's family has a little tradition called 'family legends'. Over dinner, one of the parents tells a story about their childhood. They say they have been surprised at how many family stories they can recreate for their children. It has been a great way for the children to learn more about their extended family. Sometimes our daughter thinks of something that is going on in their wee lives and tells a related story: bullies at school, not winning, sibling rivalry, name calling, or just something funny. The kids all have their favourites that they want to hear over and over again. These include Grandma running away from kindergarten, Uncle Jonny not wearing underpants to school, the night they were born, going to Waiheke on the ferry, when Mummy and Daddy fell in love . . .

Our daughter says, 'As the tradition grows the older children will probably love to add the stories they remember about their own childhood.' The five-year-old enjoys telling this story: 'Well, when I was two I was pretty naughty, and one day at the zoo I ran after the elephants and got really badly lost. A lady put me on the train and everyone was looking for me!'

'What do you think?' meals

This is a great way of teaching young children the art of conversation, and ways of sharing their ideas and opinions. Cut up 20 to 30 small pieces of paper. Write a question on each piece, fold it up and place it in a glass jar or a bowl in the middle of the table. Every few minutes pass the bowl around the table, and let someone take a turn at answering a question. Even children as young as two and three should be encouraged to volunteer their ideas. Think up questions like: If you were prime minister for a day, what three laws would you make? What was your teacher wearing today? What's the kindest thing anyone has ever done for you? What's the most delicious food you've ever tasted? What is the first thing you can ever remember, and how old do you think you were at the time? What's the best thing about being in our family?

hot tip ✪

IDEAS FOR CREATING FUN MEALTIMES

Make a customised placemat for each child — photocopy two pages of your daughter's favourite reading book or nursery rhyme (Dr Seuss is perfect), then laminate them. This is great for children between four and seven years of age who are learning to read, as they can read their story out loud at the meal table. Other ideas are:

✪ Monday manners night.

✪ Celebration meals for anytime: make special placemats, invitations, hats, etc.

✪ Picnic anywhere but at the dinner table.

✪ Tell a family legend.

Want to make mealtimes healthier?

A study by the Baylor College of Medicine in Houston, Texas, found that when kids ate with their families they ate more vegetables, drank less soft drink, and ate more foods that were lower in fat. The researchers also commented that the television set should not be invited to dinner. Focus on your time with your children, not on the tube, if you want the benefits.

The second leg of the parenting stool – monitoring systems

Then there are the rules, and the way families choose to monitor those rules. You can have a 'family rules night', and set the rules up so that everyone knows what they are. Ask for your children's input and keep the rules simple. After that they can be put up on the family noticeboard for everyone to see.

As your children get older, family mottoes and mission statements all create a sense of what you stand for as a family, and your girls will buy into the fact that they are your guidelines.

Use family rules to monitor speech. We only do 'put ups' in our family, not 'put downs'. If anyone does a put down they have to be the servant of the other person for the rest of the day and do their chores.

Use charts for short periods of time to change a behaviour. Try to keep them positive: I was gentle to the cat; I smiled and said hello to the visitors nicely, etc. After your daughter has earned five stars reward her with a small treat — maybe something like a trip to the $2 shop, or a voucher for an ice cream with Daddy.

Once a week award the red plate to someone in the family who has done something worthwhile. It may be for learning a new skill like tying her shoelaces, doing well in a test, or a quality like her kindness in giving the last cake to the visitors.

hot tip ✪

AWARDING THE RED PLATE

Every child deserves positive attention, and especially some real affirmation from siblings and parents. Each Friday night allow one family member to have their dinner on a special red plate. At Parents Inc we sell a red plate with the words 'You Are a Star — We Appreciate You'.

Just who is going to get the plate can be a surprise up to the last minute, but make a big deal about what the privilege is for. It may be that Jane has learned to tie her own shoelaces this week, that Maddie's team won their soccer game, or that Amalia got her licence. This is a really great way for children to practise both giving and receiving affirmation. It is not unusual for the children who aren't awarded the plate to cry or complain, so be prepared to run the gauntlet of a few tears if this happens!

Remember, this is an opportunity for your child to learn how to cheer and clap for someone else, and to be happy for their success. You may like to use the following saying, and perhaps put it on the fridge for a week or two: 'When something nice happens to somebody else be glad for them — not sad for yourself.'

Allowances or pocket money

Teach your daughter about money and give her ownership of managing a level of finances. Occasionally pocket money, or a part of it, may be withheld for a serious misdemeanour, but this should not be your regular means of indicating consequences.

Neale S. Godfrey, the author of *Money Doesn't Grow on Trees* and *A Penny Saved*, suggests that many values are taught through money management, or the lack of it. Girls need to be financially savvy, and you can begin with the way in which you hand out pocket money.

Godfrey's suggestion of having three jars — one for giving, one for saving, and one for spending — is a good one. She suggests giving your daughter half her age in pocket money, divided between the three labelled jars. Your daughter will then have to decide who she will give to from the giving jar. Under your guidance she might help support an orphan, or together you might have a family project on behalf of another family.

Your daughter will learn from having spending money that when it is gone, it is gone; and from her saving jar that putting aside a proportion of her allowance means she can save up for things she really wants.

Plan family excursions, and give each of your daughters a certain amount of money to plan the refreshments.

Without relaxing standards, keep the atmosphere relaxed

Probably the best thing to keep in mind is to maintain the fun and love intact, without removing the consequences of breaking family rules. Mary tells a lovely story of family friends who, with several teenage children, were rather tight financially, so they decided one year to have a 'coupon Christmas', whereby they all gave each other coupons instead of presents. The dad put together what he thought was a very creative selection of coupons for his daughter's present. He thought hard about what she hated most, so that the coupons had real value. Among them was a coupon for one tidy of her bedroom, and one 'anti-grounding' coupon! He told how he had nearly forgotten about the anti-grounding coupon until the following February when she did something really irresponsible. He was feeling frustrated and angry about her behaviour, and he said to her, 'The bad news is that I'm really mad with you, but the good news is that I am not going to talk to you about this until I have calmed down. So you are grounded for the weekend and we are going to talk about this!' His daughter looked sheepish but then sneaked into her bedroom, shuffled around in her top drawer, and came out with her anti-grounding coupon. The father told us, 'I was really frustrated, until I remembered that my wife had given me an anti-anti-grounding coupon!' These wise parents had created a home in which the boundaries meant something, but where the environment of warmth and fun kept their daughter attached and on board.

The third leg of the parenting stool — teaching character

The third leg of the parenting stool is teaching our girls values and morals, and training their character so that they grow in altruism as well as empathy. The building blocks of conscience are laid down as early as 18 months old, and again relate to a girl's attachment to and trust in her parents. As she is able to relax back into the consistent care of her parents your daughter will be able to look outside herself with courage and empathy and be taught to think about other people's feelings.

Children need to learn right and wrong and to know that the family stands for goodness. A child's inner sense of her own significance actually tells her that she is capable of doing the right thing because it is the right thing to do. It is this resonance with her good character that you as a family can affirm and build on. Your daughter will soak in your values as you talk about them and give her the reasons behind your rules.

The current generation is suffering in many ways from the lack of an objective moral compass, and girls, who traditionally were concerned about values and social interactions, have suffered the most. The modern world often tells us to use 'feelings' as a predictor of what is right and as guidelines for behaviour, especially for girls. This sort of thinking leads girls into all sorts of relationship chaos, among other things. Feelings are only feelings. They don't teach us if a course of action is right or not.

Modern, feelings-based, condom-based sex education teaches young people to ask themselves when they 'feel' ready to have sex. Girls of 14 and 15 may feel ready to have sex, but it doesn't mean that it is right, or that they are able to handle the consequences. It also doesn't mean they have thought about how their actions might affect other people like their family.

Feelings can be irrational, changeable, unpredictable and often incomprehensible. They are frequently confused with moods, which can be the result of something as simple as a bad-hair day, insufficient sleep or a bout of indigestion. As we know, feelings are a hugely unreliable guide for teenagers and when mixed with immature judgement they form a cocktail for bad decision-making.

Dr Laura Schlessinger, a top American talkback host, psychologist, and author of the book *The Ten Commandments*, says: 'An almost indiscriminate, idolatrous reverence for feelings has been one of the most insidious consequences of the field of psychology gone "pop". Though it may be therapeutic to plumb the depths of an individual's emotional confusion while "in session", having feelings become veritable temples of worship has proven disastrous for civilization.'

Dr Schlessinger tells how 'after 20 years of call-in radio, I can tell you that the main thrust of too many lives is an overemphasis on feeling good instead of doing good. Being admired and respected by the self and others has taken a back seat to feeling good or at least avoiding feeling bad.'

The mere experience of feeling is given a respectability and significance beyond its logical due. Dr Schlessinger goes on to talk about courage, character and conscience as the qualities that build a life of meaning, and how we humans are our decisions, our actions and our beliefs; that happiness is not the same as pleasure, but comes through building something worthwhile and purposeful.

Research into what builds character in children points to parents who offer clear explanations of right and wrong, and a treasury of stories to which children can relate and against which they can measure the quality of their own character. A rich soup of morality tales, historic stories of women of great courage, and more modern tales should be part of their heritage from us. As a family, develop the habit of reading together. On holiday, while cuddled up on a wet day you might read a Narnia tale, or during the winter have a regular after-dinner family reading, then together talk about what you have read and what your daughter would have done in a similar situation. Dig out books that tell stories of brave women.

In her book *Growing a Girl*, Dr Barbara Mackoff says: 'Hannah, Jeremy, and I are collecting "brave" girls. Whenever one of her friends or a character in a book or movie takes a risk, stares down a dragon, or stands up to a bully, we say, "That was a brave thing that Laura (her best friend) did." Then we add her name to a list that grew longer as Hannah grew taller: Sheila Rae (from a Kevin Henkes story), Fern (*Charlotte's Web*), Belle and Pocahontas (from Disney stories), Claudia Kincaid (*From the Mixed-Up Files of Mrs. Basil E. Frankweiler*). From time to time Hannah will announce, "I'm brave, just like Belle and Fern and Sheila Rae."'

We will capitalise on these stories about heroines with character and strength if we point out specific qualities that we admire and that our daughter can aspire to. Whenever you encounter a heroine, or a potential heroine, who makes a smart, nurturing or daring move, give that quality a name. 'Don't you love her curiosity?' 'What a loving mother she is!' 'She never gives up, does she?' 'What a resourceful way to handle that!'

As a parent, think of yourself as a coach, a manager and a resource

Being ahead of the game can affect the whole day! Be the big person. Set the agenda for the day by being proactive and organised. Even if you have to get up a few minutes earlier each day you will find it worth it in the smooth running of your family. Routines are your friend. They will save you having to reinstruct your daughter every day.

Mary remembers as a conscientious young teacher spending hours in the classroom after school, making sure that the next day was well-planned, books marked and resources in their place. This detailed organisation wasn't necessarily in her nature, but was driven by her knowledge that in order for the classroom to run smoothly and her young charges to progress through the variety of subjects that the curriculum and timetable required, this organisation was necessary.

As she became a more experienced teacher, there were days when she was not so organised — even the occasional day when she arrived just before the bell! The interesting thing is that she remembers getting to the end of those 'late-arriving' days exhausted. Not being in the classroom and organised before the children turned up just seemed to sequentially trip the atmosphere of the whole day. She says it was as if she was running to catch up, not able to get on top of things, and the children somehow were less well-behaved because of it.

Years later, she applied the same principles to parenting. With a household of active children, a busy husband and part-time work herself, she realised that it was worth the investment of getting up a few minutes earlier to set the right tone for the day.

Action lab ➤➤

Three things your girls need to thrive

Ross Campbell, in *How to Really Love Your Child*, says all children need loving eye contact, focused attention and physical closeness. However, it is significant that we often only use all these expressions of attention when we want to give an instruction or to chastise them. The same tools are far more valuable when used to express love when playing and enjoying each other.

Loving eye contact

➤➤ Make warm, loving eye contact when you are playing or taking her out for a hot chocolate.

Focused attention

➤➤ Take the time for one-on-one attention once a day; at the end of the bed, after school over a snack or when taking her with you on an outing. Listen to her 'Yays' and her 'Yucks': the positive and negative things. Listening is the language of love.

Physical affection

➤➤ It's incredible what a meaningful and appropriate touch, hug, embrace, kiss, or even a gentle back-rub will do to a young person's self-image. Touching brings a real sense of meaningfulness and security.

Finally, let her play

Want to help your child excel? Then let her play. According to the American Academy of Pediatrics, many kids are overwhelmed by activities geared towards turning them into super-achievers. But an important part of a child's development is simply playing.

Unstructured playtime will help your daughter develop imagination, creativity and problem-solving skills, and let her discover her own interests. So encourage her to go through your kitchen cabinets, dig for worms in the backyard, or play with your old jewellery. You don't need a week full of structured activities to raise successful children — and you may even find the calmer schedule is better for you too.

A family that offers lots of fun, communication and celebration is on the right track. When girls begin to suffer emotionally, the answer can nearly always be found in more family closeness: more family nights; more Dad- or Mum-and-daughter nights; more time with a grandparent; family games nights, camping trips, reunions or expeditions. These are the things that create community and love for your daughter. The web of relationships provided by godparents, aunties and mentors reinforces this circle of belonging for her.

The culture of our times dictates that parents invest more

> The values they instilled in us, like treating others the way you would like to be treated ... the way you treated your brothers and sisters ... There was a consistency in Mum and Dad's life — so I could see that they practised what they were teaching us ... There wasn't one set of rules for them and another set of rules for us ... they were living things like looking out for others.
>
> **— Jess**, *20*

Before we began this book we talked to a variety of fine young women displaying confidence, autonomy, empathy, leadership and ability in their chosen careers. Throughout the book we quote these young women, because their observations offer significant insights.

In 2006 the Barna Group, a market research firm that specialises in studying the religious beliefs and behaviour of Americans, conducted a study of families who had passed on their values and their faith to their children. When we compare their results with the lives of the girls we interviewed there are some definite parallels. In all of the families, the parents made parenting a priority and were prepared to invest time during the crucial years. Today's children and teens are wise beyond their years. The days of complete innocence have gone. Children are growing up with social issues, drugs, racial problems, environmental concerns and many others. And the roles of parents and children no longer follow traditional patterns. Seventy per cent of mothers now work full- or part-time, compared with only 30 per cent in the 1980s, making it harder to stay in touch.

Self-absorption is rampant in today's society, and encouraging unbridled self-analysis can only serve to make this worse. Healthy, functioning families and communities rely on people being able to see that they are part of a bigger picture, one that does not revolve around them.

The 'it's all about me' culture doesn't create happiness. Psychologists have now concluded that the emphasis on how the child feels has led to a fixation with the self which paradoxically increases the likelihood of depression and anxiety. Many suggest taking alternative measures to improve the well-being of children, focusing more on service, such as taking action and 'doing things in the world'.

hot tip ✪

- Decide what you stand for as a family. Make service to others something you do together, and commit to as a family.
- Create a family life that is rich in stories and tales of character. Keep reading and telling stories about heroines. Give your daughter role models, and affirm qualities you admire in them in your day-to-day speech.
- Teach your daughter that feelings have a place, but that they don't always tell the truth. Tell her how proud you are of her when she does the right thing, shows kindness or trustworthiness.
- Make mealtimes a highlight. Take a few minutes to plan a 'different' context or focus and it will pay off in the enjoyment as well as the memories.
- Share jokes, exchange news, relate family anecdotes and laugh at mistakes. Be positive with your daughter so that she sees you as a relaxed, outgoing person – not just a tense, serious parent.

in summary ✏

WHAT GIRLS NEED TO THRIVE

Girls need a family in which:
- They are valued as members of a team.
- There is lots of conversation and connection.
- Fun and communication are part of the family culture.
- Boundaries and discipline are monitored.
- Character and virtues are taught.
- Parents are the big people person – coach, manager and resource.
- They have a chance to play.

Chapter 7

Love and limits

It's not the severity of the consequences, but the certainty of them that matters. Give your child ownership of the problem, the tools to solve it and leave her dignity intact.

— **Barbara Coloroso,** Kids Are Worth It!

All of us work for payoffs at some level. That's just human nature. What constitutes a payoff varies from one person to another. As the old saying goes, one man's trash is another man's treasure. It is for that reason that you must empirically define whether a given consequence is truly positive for your child.

— **Dr Phil McGraw,** Family First

The magic in your children's lives is likely to come from the fun and playfulness in your family life, but parents also have to master the art of setting limits on behaviour and teaching their daughters how to operate happily and confidently in the world. These are the two sides of parenting, and it is sometimes a challenge to achieve a balance. Really understanding your daughter, knowing her nature and getting behind her 'eyes' will increase your ability to parent her. It will also provide you both with an easier road as she takes on the task of becoming a cooperative part of the family and wider community.

Just as a coach studies and maximises each individual player's strengths, you can work with your daughter's individual personality and nature to gain cooperation and build trust. All children feel more secure when there are rules and boundaries along with a lot of love and affection. It is important to remember that children can be both selfish and power-seeking. This is not a deliberate ploy on their part to frustrate parents; they are just human beings looking to get their needs and wants met.

We adults often ignore the fact that children are still just children, and that they can't be expected to reflect and think through situations as an adult would. Because of the developmental stage they are at, they tend to reflect the world as they find it — mostly through what they see and hear from their parents. It is our role to be in charge, and to lead them from the early egocentricity of toddler-hood towards the recognition that other people have thoughts and feelings about what they do and say, and finally to lead them to think before acting. This needs to be done in an age-appropriate way as they progress through to maturity and self-discipline.

The most positive homes are those in which both warmth and structure surround the children. As a parent you need to be secure in your own mind about the value of both love and limits. You will need to see yourself as both a coach and a cheerleader in your daughter's life. In other words, you will always be 'in her corner' no matter what happens; not rescuing her necessarily, but backing her, training her in life skills, and after a setback showing her how to get off the bench and back into the game of life. Your goal always, in setting limits and remaining firm but friendly, is to love her unconditionally and bring out the best in her.

Your daughter and discipline

It is very important that you clearly decide on a philosophy of parenting. If you don't, it is likely that you will find yourselves parenting reactively as situations arise. When children do foolish, 'childish' things that upset you, you sometimes take it personally rather than take charge as the big people they need to teach them, coach them, set consequences and restore their sense of worth. Your own emotions and wiring kick in and you are likely to fall into patterns that are familiar from your own childhoods.

If you come from a yelling family, then yelling may make you feel better when your daughter breaks something precious. But it will not necessarily teach her anything about obedience or respecting property. In fact, the emotion you exude with the yelling is likely to do the opposite. While she is dealing with the anger you emanate she will not be able to think clearly about what she should have done. Instead she may be being programmed to become sneaky, defensive and manipulative if she is more aware of your anger than the fact that she has done something wrong.

For your child to learn lessons from your parenting, you will need more resources than just yelling, telling off or lectures.

When your small daughter helps herself to a jug of juice from the refrigerator and spills it over the floor, you can either yell at her, telling her what a stupid, naughty or wasteful thing she has done, or you can take the approach of a good coach with a player who has made a 'blue'. Look disappointed and firm, get down beside her, offer her a cloth and a bowl — give her the tools to put it right. You may have to help her, but as a coach you have a long-term goal in mind, which is to show her how to take responsibility for her actions and how to put them right. We do not want our children to be afraid of our anger, but to know that if they make a mistake or do something wrong they can take responsibility for their actions and help put it right.

During the course of each day your child is learning that life is a series of 'yesses' and 'noes'. 'Yes, we can go to the park after we tidy the toys'; 'No, you can't have a biscuit just now, but you may have a slice of apple or a cheese stick.'

Discipline is about teaching your daughter good social skills, a sense of right and wrong, and self-discipline. Children are happier when there are definite limits and they have a clear understanding of acceptable behaviour. Bringing up children without discipline is like sailing a ship without a rudder.

Develop a style of parenting that helps you enjoy living with your child. And try to work out ahead of time answers to the following questions, as appropriate for the age of your child:

• What happens if my daughter does something wrong?

• What happens if she does something right?

United parenting

As long as both parents live in the same house, the most important principle you can follow is united parenting. Your daughter will thrive on the security this offers, and will suffer if she smells the lack of a united front from her parents.

Unfortunately, what sometimes happens when one parent is perceived as too controlling or tough is that the other parent becomes even softer as a way of compensating. This in turn sets up a see-saw effect with one parent becoming more strict while the other becomes more permissive. It is very much in both your interests to back each other up. And if you do feel that the other parent is being too tough, or too soft, don't have the discussion in front of your child.

One couple who realised the effect this sort of dissonance was having on their children tried to break the pattern, and in so doing changed the whole atmosphere in their home. As the wife resisted the urge to censor her husband in front of the children for being too strict, and just backed him silently, then he began to change. Previously, when he had insisted the children each tidy their own rooms before breakfast she had fought him (and tried to modify his high expectations), with the result that he had become even tougher and less open to negotiation. As she changed her habits, he felt secure in the fact that she was supporting him (if only by not opposing him) and became more relaxed. He remained firm but became more fair and somewhat more friendly.

Create a climate for united parenting by honouring each other, showing affection in front of the children, and greeting each other with love and warmth. Mum's let your children know that you have a huge amount of respect for their dad, and when he is not present speak positively about him. Tell them what a wonderful father he is, and mention things he does without being noticed, as well as the fun stuff he does. In the same way, dads, honour your wife. Think of her as a treasure in your home, refuse to allow disrespectful language, and compliment her at every opportunity

— and your children will take on your view of her.

The greatest thing a father can do for his daughter is to love her mother. If a child swears at or verbally abuses your spouse, or says 'I hate you', the consequence is non-negotiable. What you are communicating is that this person is of great value, and if you show disrespect for them you have stepped over a line.

hot tip ✪

Even if you don't live with the father or mother of your child, you will not help your daughter by speaking disrespectfully about her other parent. Where possible, make a point of honouring them. Remember, you made a daughter together. That will never change.

Unfortunately, parents these days are sometimes so busy trying to manage their lives that they will overlook a disrespectful incident because they want to keep the atmosphere happy. A distressed couple recently talked to a friend whose eight-year-old daughter had sworn at her mother on the way to a family outing to the zoo. The father ignored the outburst because he didn't want to spoil the excursion, which had been especially chosen by the girl, and which everyone had been looking forward to. Unwittingly, he had thereby given his daughter permission to continue with this sort of behaviour.

Children often choose inappropriate times to test your boundaries. If you don't respond immediately — turn the car around and deliver her back home because she has crossed a boundary — then this behaviour will happen again.

Sometimes we have to face short-term pain for long-term gain. If you set a consequence or family rule, then you have to be prepared to follow through. Otherwise your children will not take you seriously.

Unfortunately, if you are working to change a pattern of behaviour you will have to learn to put on your parenting 'hard hat' if your daughter, upset about the new regime, throws a tantrum, slams doors or gives you the silent treatment. You need to remain convinced that the consequence, as long as it is logical and reasonable, will have its effect. Your calm resolve will mean that things will settle down — the consequence will work and 'compliance' will become your daughter's problem, not yours.

The golden rule of discipline is establish the ABC before you get to the D of discipline.

A =   *The atmosphere in your home should be loving, affirming and fun.*

B =   *The boundaries are clearly explained and established.*

C =   *Lots of positive communication and coaching from parents.*

The number one rule of parenting is to establish compliance in the small things that matter in your family, like manners and cooperation with family routines. That early compliance will be the building block of good behaviour later.

We don't mean that you should be on your daughter's back over every little thing; in fact, the opposite should be true. Most of your interactions should be affirming and encouraging, but do be sure to be firm about those few things that really matter. Yes, you can let your daughter choose to wear the pink dress with the yellow top to kindy, rather than the cerise one that you like — but make sure you retain the decision about what she wears when you go to church or lunch with friends on Sunday. Mind you, even that decision could have an element of choice; for instance, 'This pile of clothes or that one.'

It is likely that every little girl will test even this boundary at some stage, and this is when you will have to be firm and perhaps a little wise. Zoe's exchange with her father is an example:

Father: 'You may wear either the blue dress or the green one, which one is it?'

Daughter: 'I want to wear the purple one!'

'Well that actually isn't one of the choices, sweetheart. You can wear the blue dress or the green one.'

'I want to wear the purple one with the pink buttons!'

'I'm afraid then we have a problem, because the purple dress is in the wash and it isn't an option. Now, we have to go out that door in 10 minutes, so you can wear either of these two dresses or you can come in your pyjamas. I'll just go and finish getting ready and you can decide.'

When it came to the crunch, Zoe capitulated, but her father may have had to be prepared to carry through the promise of the outing in her pyjamas . . . if only once!

Yes, you can offer her choices between two flavours of ice cream or what type of pizza she wants, but make sure you give your child age-appropriate choices, and preferably two choices rather than three or four. If, early in her life, she is allowed to make all the decisions about what she eats, wears or does, you are not only going to grow an insecure child but you are going to have a very hard time winding back some control when she is a teenager. When your daughter is little you have most of the control, and your parenting responsibility will involve a journey of giving her more and more age-appropriate levels of control and choice as she grows.

Remember that rules for young children should be simple: 'We don't hurt others, we don't hurt things, we don't hurt ourselves'; 'We smile and welcome visitors'; 'We do what Mummy and Daddy say the first time.' And it is these very rules that will give your child the early security she needs to understand the world.

> Parenting and playfulness can seem like contradictions, but sometimes we just need a little push to find each other and have fun together.
>
> **– Dr Lawrence Cohen,** Playful Parenting

Write up the family rules together

You will have to discipline your children far less if you have rules in place. Most children will accept a rule if it is stated without fuss. For instance, it is very easy to monitor a rule when you can say, for example, 'Remember, that's our rule, we only have half an hour of screen time.' Or, 'The rule is that everyone has to wash their hands and be up at the table before we start the meal. You have one minute — quick, see if you can beat the timer!' 'The rule about bikes and scooters is that you put them away before dinner time.'

Your motivation in disciplining is to guide her to make better choices

Discipline your daughter without anger, with your motivation being to help her to make better choices in future — the consequences will do the teaching. Consequences are a far better teacher than your anger or your lecture.

So stay on your child's side against the problem, and empathise with her over the consequences. For instance, 'What a shame you left your bike out — it's going to have to go away until the weekend.' 'Remember the rule — your best shoes were left in the rain, they will have to go into the Saturday box and you will have to wait until then to wear them again,' 'I asked you to stop doing that. Remember the rule — I'm afraid that will have to be half an hour earlier to bed!'

The key for parents is to stay calm when your child is upset. Your daughter is not likely to enjoy it when a consequence kicks in, and you may have to steel yourself against your own reluctance to create drama if she decides to do battle. You will only need to follow through once or twice on a consequence before she realises that it is not you she is fighting but the consequences that she sets herself.

'I must feel and think about others before I do something'

With girls you can use 'inductive discipline'; in other words you can ask them how they would feel if someone did that to them. This is much harder with boys, as boys are likely to hear 'What would you *do* if . . .?' when you ask them how they would feel.

Allow your daughter to fail in small ways, so that she experiences the consequences of those failures. Positive parents teach their children reasoning skills. You need to give them the freedom to choose, and then to sink or swim, as long as it is a failure that is not life-endangering or morally threatening. For example, if they spend all their pocket money, there is none left until next payday. If they leave their lunch behind, there may be one free delivery per term, but after that they will go hungry.

As they head into adolescence our style of discipline changes and we will influence more than control.

Discipline should be firm, fair and friendly

Many parents think they can make their child feel so bad or so guilty or so ashamed about something, she won't ever do it again. Unfortunately that doesn't work. Yes, it may produce shame and guilt and even a certain level of compliance, but it is not going to help them make a better choice next time, or to let them know that they can think for themselves.

Therefore, as a coach the way you handle discipline is to support your child, but address the behaviour. You don't need to be embarrassed about your parenting skills if your child decides to misbehave in the supermarket or a restaurant. Don't take personally what your child does. It is not what she does that matters, it is how you respond. Swiftly scooping up a toddler, taking her out into the carpark and sitting her somewhere safe for two minutes' thinking time can do the trick.

A few years ago Mary and I were holidaying in Noosa. While eating at a restaurant we observed an incident in which a dad responded superbly to his tantrumming child without allowing her to spoil the meal for everyone else. At the next table a little girl sitting with her family began to make a fuss about the French fries. She started by whining, and then when her parents tried to placate her, she threw all her chips on the floor. While trying to stay focused on my meal, I whispered to Mary: 'Here is some research, right in front of us!'

The father immediately picked up his daughter, without showing any embarrassment or anger, and carried her out of the restaurant. A few moments later I needed to visit the restroom, and on my way back I passed the father sitting with his daughter on the steps. I heard him say quietly, 'When you are ready to behave, we will go back in and join the family.' A few minutes later we watched as he returned with his smiling daughter, and the meal continued without further incident.

When your young daughter refuses to do as she is told, then you can tell her that you will 'wait' until she is ready — whether it is to say hello nicely to Grandma or to behave in the supermarket. If she yells for lollies in the supermarket, you can tell her lollies are only for parties, or try to distract her, but if this doesn't work you may need to take her back to the car and strap her in her car seat for a few minutes while you wait outside or sit quietly in the front seat. You are giving her the message that you are in charge and this tantrum is not working.

Have rewards in place for when she behaves nicely in the supermarket, such as a jelly snake or a voucher for a picnic in the garden.

The key is that you are showing her how to behave. When she doesn't get it right, help her by practising, and don't forget to reward her with your words or hugs when she responds correctly.

Cue, prompt and reinforce

- Cue — before you leave home, remind your child what is going to happen. Let her practise what she will do when she gets there — like tiptoeing quietly when you are off to visit Grandad in hospital.
- Prompt — prompt her as you arrive. 'Remember our quiet voices and tippy toes. Can you show me?'
- Reinforce — when she does as you wish, praise her, especially in front of Grandad when you reach his room.

Don't let your child's behaviour embarrass you. The father in the story above took charge and acted as the big person, therefore handling the situation well. And don't delay your action and allow the behaviour to wind up.

The ebbing tide of parental authority

Sociologist Norbert Elias is regarded by many experts as one of the great social critics of our modern age. Towards the end of his life he developed a thesis to do with the transfer of authority from parents to children. It went something like this. Fifty years ago a parent would tell their daughter which high school she was going to attend. Today, parents consult with their daughter. They might suggest or even beg, but the final decision will be with the girl. The result of this loss of parental authority, to use the phrase coined by Dr Elias, is 'status uncertainty', and it gives a parent insecurity over what authority they have over their children.

In modern society, the relocation of power from parent to child has resulted in an 'informalisation' of relations between the generations, to the extent that some children address their parents, and their parents' friends, by their first names. While this makes it easier for parents to be friends with their children, it also makes it harder for parents to be parents. According to Dr Elias, it causes a feeling of uncertainty and leaves parents 'at sea without a compass'. A friendship is a reciprocal relationship between social peers. The parent–child relationship is not a reciprocal relationship between peers, nor should it be.

This 'informalisation' of relations also puts an unfair burden on a child, because she is often expected to have a level of wisdom and maturity that developmentally she is not ready for. Little kids are very literal, and they don't always know what they think or feel, or what is best for them. They will even tell us what they think we want to hear.

Girls rarely begin to have in-depth understanding of their thoughts, feelings and motivations before late adolescence. The process develops through adults pushing them to link logical consequences with actions. This helps them move from the more 'concrete thinking' of childhood towards the 'formal' thinking of adulthood.

Sylvia Rimm's 'V of love'

Psychologist and educator Sylvia Rimm has a wonderful principle that will stand you in good stead when parenting your daughter. She calls it the 'V of love'. It is based on the idea that once given power human beings will rarely give it up without a struggle. However, the corollary is that children are usually satisfied with the amount of power they have, as long as they know they are progressing towards a greater amount. As your children grow up you will be able to add gradually to their choices and their power. So little children begin at the base of the V.

The bottom of the V of love represents parents' rules. When children are young they have little freedom and few choices. As they get older, you will begin to widen the V to give them more freedom and more choices. Finally, in late adolescence, you are moving towards the top of the V and most of your parenting involves negotiation within the much wider V of your authority.

When your daughter is two years old, you as parents will have a lot of control, and she will not have a lot of choices. For instance, you will decide that she must wear something on her feet, she may eat an apple, and she must wear pyjamas. However, the detail can be offered as a choice to your daughter. She may choose whether to wear her sandals or her crocs; whether to have the red apple or the yellow one, and what colour pyjamas to wear.

As a seven-year-old you make the rule that she must play a sport, but she can choose what sport she plays. As she gets older your boundaries are still in place, but there is more room for trust and negotiation about how she chooses within those guidelines.

Work with your daughter's natural desire to please you

- Use connection, not separation, to bring a child into line.
- When problems occur, work the relationship, not the incident.
- When things aren't working for your child, draw out the tears instead of trying to teach a lesson. (If you are stuck in a power struggle, this approach can bring you much closer than endless standoffs.)

Address dishonesty or misbehaviour firmly but lovingly

Don't overlook misbehaviour. Lay out the problem for your child, give her a way to help solve the problem, and leave her dignity intact. For instance, 'Now look, you've been jumping on the bed. This is not the playroom. Our rule is no jumping in the guestroom. Now what do you need to do to fix it? . . . I'll be in the kitchen – come and tell me when you've put it right.'

Action lab ➤➤

FIRM FAIR FRIENDLY RULES FOR PARENTS

We can be firm about:

➤➤ *Values, such as honesty and courtesy;*

➤➤ *Respect and safety for self, others and property;*

➤➤ *Follow–through.*

We can be fair by:

➤➤ *Being prepared to listen and to re-evaluate unreasonable decisions;*

➤➤ *Acknowledging that different treatment of different children is often appropriate (e.g. adjusting bedtimes according to age and stage);*

➤➤ *Setting consequences that are logical and reasonable;*

➤➤ *Loving unconditionally without favouritism.*

We can be friendly by:

➤➤ *Disciplining without anger or violence;*

➤➤ *Helping our child to develop a plan to avoid the problem next time;*

➤➤ *Staying calm; being deliberate in our tone of voice, choice of words, timing and body language;*

➤➤ *Avoiding power-struggles by using 'fighting words'.*

By learning to make her bed your daughter will save her brain

It's true. Dr Robert Wilson, author of a groundbreaking study at Rush University, Chicago, says conscientious people have less chance of developing Alzheimer's disease, and conscientiousness can start with parents teaching their children how to make their beds. This is just another good reason for parents to put in place healthy structures and discipline in their home.

Although you may not be thinking this far into your daughter's future, Dr Wilson suggests that hard-working, goal-oriented and dependable people have a lower risk of getting Alzheimer's disease. He defines conscientiousness as, 'I keep my belongings clean, I pace myself to get things done on time, I have a clear set of goals, I work towards them in an orderly fashion.' In an interview in *Newsweek* he suggests that for this reason parents should encourage their children to do their homework promptly, and make their beds, reinforcing the value of teamwork and responsibility.

You don't have to say yes or no – try 'Convince me!'

Barbara Coloroso, the author of *Kids Are Worth It!* and *The Bully, the Bullied and the Bystander*, is well known for her work in teaching kids responsibility and ownership. She first discussed this strategy with me during an interview on Newstalk ZB. I hand it on to all parents of teenagers as it will stand you in good stead over many issues. This is how Barbara Coloroso explained it:

'If your teenager asks, "Can I have the car?" a reply I use with a teenager is "Convince me." In fact, you can use this with anyone who is verbal. And she says, "But Mum all my friends . . ." and you say, "I'm not convinced." "But Mum, you let Maria." "I'm not convinced." "Mum, if you don't let me have the car keys, you're going to have to take every one of us to play practice." "I'm convinced!"

'Many people say "No" far too often. If you don't say it a lot and give your kids options and choices, they will learn that these things are negotiable, that you're all in the family together. Mum and Dad are the adults though, and they will say "No" when they really need to.'

hot tip ⊙

FOCUS ON CHARACTER

Make a habit of commenting positively on character traits that you value in your family. Try something like this: 'That shows real creativity', or 'I admire the determination you have shown over that.' This simple focus tips the balance back towards what is truly important.

Inspire your daughter with stories and people

Although this chapter is really about discipline, the other side of the coin is that you want your daughter to have ideals to look up to, including what you stand for as a family. One young woman I spoke to recently said, 'You know my parents were really firm and I sometimes thought that they were the worst parents in the world. They were certainly stricter than some of my friends' parents. But I knew that they lived by the standards that they set for us. They were always thinking of other people and putting themselves out in order to do the right thing, and that made me want to be like them. They also made sure that if they had to say no about something like drinking or parties they gave me reasons, and they always looked for an alternative, or a way to not make me feel really left out and different. They always made our house a place that my friends loved coming to. In fact, some of my friends thought our place was the coolest because of the yummy food Mum always put on, and Dad was always so welcoming.'

Look for a variety of ways to inspire your family. Invite discussions about outstanding women who have contributed to the world — women like Florence Nightingale, Kate Sheppard, Mother Teresa, Gladys Aylward (featured in *The Small Woman* and *The Inn of Sixth Happiness*), Whina Cooper, and contemporary women who show dignity and self-discipline along with all the best qualities of being a woman. Read their stories together at the dinner table, include your sons and discuss the decisions these women had to make in their lives and how those decisions affected others.

Let your daughter know you're all on the same side

Let her know that she can tell you everything, and that you will always work together on the problem — gang up on the problem, not on your daughter. When there is a problem, use words like, 'Have you any ideas? How could we work this out?' Alternatively, 'What a shame, what will you need to do to make things better?' or 'I'm sure you can handle it — if you need me, let me know.'

Try to be home after school, or have someone there who cares about your daughter

When she gets home from school this can be your chance to debrief and let her unload. Things that may depress, alarm or just worry her will be put in perspective after unloading and a chat with a loving adult.

Take control of the environment into which your daughter arrives home. Happy music creates its own atmosphere. A vase of daisies on the table and a hot drink, or muffins or fresh bread popped in the oven, create a warm, welcoming atmosphere and give you a head start in reconnecting as your daughter arrives home. Make a decision to greet her with delight and a smile. The first words she hears will create a feeling of responsiveness or defensiveness. Atmosphere and even aromas create a haven.

hot tip ✪

- Remember your daughter is not trying to get at you; she is just a child without internal limits or controls. Be the big person.
- If possible, give your daughter reasons for family rules: 'In our house we don't jump on chairs because they get broken.'
- If today's rules are different, tell her the reason: 'We are expecting visitors. I don't want toys in the lounge this morning. Please keep them in your room.'
- If you want your daughters to have boundaries then ensure that you act as a role model and turn off the TV when your programme is over, read quietly for an evening, spend money wisely.
- With young children you can use marbles or pocket money in a jar as rewards or as consequences. One system is to put 50 cents a day in 10-cent coins in a jar – withdraw coins for bad behaviour and allow her to earn them back with improvement.

in summary ✎

WHAT GIRLS NEED

Girls need parents who:

- Provide definite limits and a clear understanding of acceptable behaviour.
- Establish logical and reasonable consequences if limits are violated.
- Make consequences immediate and inevitable. A rule that is not important enough to enforce is not a rule at all.
- Discipline their daughter with a view to bringing out the best in her.
- Teach her about right and wrong, good social skills and self-discipline; model good manners, standards and self-discipline.
- Isolate the behaviour they don't want; practise the behaviour they do want; praise their daughter when she gets it right.

Chapter 8

The middle years

If you are planning for a year, sow rice. If you are planning for a decade, plant trees. If you are planning for a lifetime, educate people.

— **Chinese proverb**

Our children do not need a makeover, they just need to be understood. If you understand their emotional needs now, you can save them a lifetime of searching for what they never had as a child.

— **Florence Littauer,** Personality Plus

We believe that girls are not inherently cruel, and although behaviors such as jealousy, gossiping, and joining cliques may be normal in terms of what we expect, they are not what we have to accept. Based on our work with hundreds of young women, in both our professional and personal lives, as well as extensive research . . . we know not only can girls be kind, they feel better about themselves when they are. We call this behaviour 'confident kindness', because the ability to be caring and supportive of others is only meaningful if it comes from an inner sense of security and self-esteem.

— **Cheryl Dellasega and Charisse Nixon,** Girl Wars

The primary-school years provide a wonderful window of opportunity in which to build on your daughter's sense of confidence and encourage her to develop skills. These years tend to be more straightforward than the earlier years, as you have left toddler-hood behind and your daughter is able to exercise a certain level of independence.

School age girls tend to like black and white rules, and be open to learning what is right and wrong from you, her teachers and other adults. This is when she will come home from school and say, 'It must be right because Miss Jones said so!' She will also be learning how to develop friendships and get on with others, and a 'can do' attitude is often a hallmark of this age group. These are the years for music lessons and team sports, and your opportunity to teach her a sense of her self-worth. For more on this, see chapter 4, 'Daughters and self-esteem'.

Because life now becomes easier in lots of ways, without the power struggles of the preschool years, mothers often return to careers and as parents we may metaphorically sit back, settling into managing school routines. Life seems to be more straightforward, as we take our daughter to dance classes or sporting events, and support her in her schoolwork.

But these years provide an opportunity for so much more. This is your chance to really have input into her character, to build the memories and rituals, and to offer her an understanding of the sacredness and the wonder of life. The investment you make in these years will also make the teenage years that follow so much smoother. We often talk about this in white-water rafting terms, as 'the quiet part of the river' before the rapids ahead. This is when you can offer your child a 'garment of values' — she may later unravel and reknit it for herself, but it is when you can proactively teach her the substance of those values.

> When you are influenced by your parents you just want to be like them.
>
> — **Kate**, *17*

Your family will also be a cradle of creativity for your daughter as you encourage ideas and initiative. Make one child responsible for a family-night discussion, and suggest she puts flowers on the table and a question under each person's plate. Let her choose the menu and help to prepare the food.

Our own children remember, especially from those years, how we made breakfasts together a priority. At the breakfast table we read a short Bible story, which was followed by two or three questions and a chat about their day before we all went in our various directions. Our daughter still points to those breakfasts as a highlight of her childhood. And they had so many other spin-offs as well. They gave us a short respite in which to catch our breath before we left the house, and they sent our children off each morning with a sense of support and positive feelings.

I often kept the children 'on their toes' during the storytime by adding bits about our family into the tale. I would ask our youngest, still a preschooler, a question he couldn't fail to answer, like the name of our dog. Yes, a routine like this may mean getting up half an hour earlier, and it may be impractical in many families, but if you make 'connection time' a priority it is amazing how you can make it work. I decided that I would go for my run earlier than I had been doing, and that I would take responsibility for breakfast while Mary, who protests that she is not a morning person, was able to supervise the making of beds and the children's morning routines.

Passing on traditions takes an investment of time and effort, and will need to be structured into your week if you are serious about doing it. Recently it was reported that New Zealanders currently work some of the longest hours in the world. We have huge empathy with parents who must work such long hours just to put a roof over the heads of their children. But we also encourage you to think about how marriages and family life survive so much better if parents can reduce their working hours and keep at least one day a week for their family. Perhaps lengthening some of your financial goals and driving an older car for a while longer would allow you to capitalise on these significant years with your daughter.

It is between the ages of seven and 15, peaking at 13, that children are most receptive to learning values and beliefs. They develop their 'moral compass', their sense of right and wrong, at this age, and it seldom alters as they grow older. Most will not significantly alter their moral outlook and religious beliefs after their teenage years.

Create intentional family teaching times

Hopefully your children will pick up many of your values by watching you, but we parents also need to communicate ideals and stories that embody virtues we want emulated. A child's mind is like a garden; if we plant and nurture the good beliefs and expectations, and the attitudes we wish to grow, there will be less space for the weeds to take root. Positive teaching can prevent the establishment of so many bad attitudes and behaviours. The old adage is really true: 'Sow a thought and you reap an act, sow an act and you reap a habit, sow a habit and you reap a character, sow a character and you reap a destiny.'

Jim Weidman of Focus on the Family, who has developed some great resources for family times, suggests that the inheritance we give our children falls into three areas: a spiritual legacy; a social and relational legacy, and an emotional legacy. He emphasises the fact that we don't have to repeat our own upbringing. By making some positive decisions and rethinking what we are doing as parents we can rebuild the DNA of our home and life. The home you create is your daughter's relational heritage, she is learning from you respect and obedience, and you are modelling how a family works for her.

Jim talks about traditions that identify your family, giving kids a sense of who they are and what they belong to, and how they move a child through the maturation process. He suggests that values can best be passed on in context, and uses the acronym AROMA: affection, respect, order, merriment and affirmation. These things create the loving and harmonious environment of a home that lingers in a child's heart for a lifetime. Without it, rather than accepting and absorbing your values and faith, children are more likely to react against them.

When children are having fun they learn naturally, and some structure just makes the whole thing work. To explain what Jim Weidman is suggesting, here's an example of a typical family night based on Focus on the Family's 'Family night tool chest', which teaches about the power of words and how they affect others. Over their lifetimes girls will have many challenges when relational aggression and verbal tactics are used by other girls, so equip them early with the attitudes you want them to develop.

Action lab ➵

FAMILY NIGHT ON THE POWER OF WORDS

An activity:

➵ *Have the children sit around the dinner table. Give each of them a small tube of toothpaste and a paper plate. Have them race to squeeze every possible drop of toothpaste out of the tube onto the plate. Give them two or three minutes to finish the job. When done, give them each a spoon, lay a $10 note on the table, and tell them that the first person to get all of the toothpaste back into the tube wins the money. Give them twice as long to finish — four to six minutes. (Don't worry, your money is safe.)*

Pose questions:

➵ *Which was harder, squeezing the toothpaste out or trying to get it back in?*

Point:

➵ *Once the words are out of our mouths we can never take them back. Just as the toothpaste came from inside the tube through the 'mouth' of the tube, so our words come out from inside our hearts and minds through our mouths. What's in our heart controls what's on our mind, and what's on our mind controls what we say. We can use our words to build up others or to pull them down.*

Takeaway:

➵ *Words to learn: 'Treat others the way you would like to be treated.'*

Take time to really understand your daughter

Understanding your child, or indeed anyone in your life, is the work of a lifetime. However, even if you just observe some personality traits and acquire some simple insights into how your daughter is 'wired' you will ensure she feels understood. It will also help you avoid personality clashes and power struggles during times of stress.

For instance, if your daughter is an introvert or an extrovert she will either resonate with you if that is your natural personality bent, or she will take some time to understand if her nature is the opposite to yours. If she is an extrovert she will tend to tell you everything that is going on, make lots of friends easily and share her ideas at the drop of a hat. If she is an introvert, getting her to share or be sociable on cue may be harder.

Most people have a basic understanding of these terms: extroverts are outgoing, chatty, expressive, and thrive in a group situation; introverts, on the other hand, are quiet, reflective, and enjoy one-on-one conversations. While these generalisations are true, there is a little more to add.

The gap between an extrovert thinking something and speaking that thought is very short: an extrovert thinks out loud. In a dialogue an extrovert may well have changed her opinion between the beginning and the end of the conversation. She will often interrupt as an idea comes into her head, and if there is a gap in the conversation she will feel compelled to fill it.

In contrast, an introvert will want to reflect on a thought and will only speak her mind once that thought has been processed. Introverts think before they speak. Their internal 'head talk' is an important part of their world, and they rely on it to form their opinions, which will only be voiced when they are ready. Introverts who understand this about themselves will be less concerned about the chatty extroverts who attract more attention.

If you as a parent also understand this, you will make sure that your introvert daughter is given opportunities to contribute around the dinner table — saying what she thinks, feels and wants — as well as her more talkative siblings. She may need more space or time to get her thoughts out. Use the family salt shaker or pepper mill as the 'talking stick' around the dinner table, letting everyone take turns to hold it and contribute to the conversation, even the youngest.

Your daughter may need you to practise a special type of listening that involves simply mirroring her thoughts, so that she learns to listen to her inner world. As you reflect and interpret her feelings to her, she will learn to trust her own observations. You might just learn to use the phrases, 'It sounds like . . .' or, 'It seems as if . . .' when you are listening to her.

Each personality type has its different needs, and understanding these opens the doors to good communication.

An extrovert needs:

- opportunities for expression;
- open communication;
- quick responses without long pauses;
- action; and
- groups.

An introvert needs:

- time to think before responding;
- quiet time to concentrate;
- no interruptions;
- one-to-one or small-group discussion; and
- advance notice of a discussion topic.

As one mother told me: 'My eight-year-old daughter would come home looking grumpy and tired, and it was only after some time in her bedroom that she would appear and tell me something that had happened at school. I kept asking her why she didn't invite her friend over to play, and in the end she said very firmly, "I just want to be on my own for a while." At that point I realised that her introverted personality had been overloaded with all the social interaction from the day, and she needed some downtime to regain her equilibrium.'

Know your daughter's love language

A number of books have been written on the subject of love languages, the most well-known by Dr Gary Chapman (see reading list at the end of this book). The basic principles are simple: there are five different ways in which we can both give and receive love, and each of us tends to have a preference. Knowing this preference helps us understand how our loved ones appreciate being acknowledged and how they feel the most loved. A child may not feel particularly loved by you if you are not spending quality time with them, whereas you as a parent may think that you are expressing your love for them by buying them gifts or praising them.

The love languages have been identified as:

- hugs;
- praise;
- time;
- gift-giving; and
- acts of service.

Whichever is our preferred way of receiving love tends to be the language in which we give it to others. If your daughter is always wrapping up little gifts for you or her siblings, then her language of love is likely to be gift-giving; you will make her feel very loved by occasionally bringing home a small gift as a surprise. Other children long for praise, some need lots of hugs and cuddles, while still others love you to do things with them. While all children deserve all these gifts of love from their parents, there is an underlying skill in knowing your daughter and understanding her nature. If you have studied her carefully you will be able to respond to her sensitively, in a way that makes her know she is loved, by operating in her love language.

Introduce these love languages to your family. Describe each one clearly and ask your children which they prefer, as well as which they think their close friends and family prefer. From about the age of six onwards your daughter is very likely to be able to state her preference. Prepare to be amazed . . . it may not always be for gifts! As a child our daughter loved nothing more than quality time spent with her, and even though as a teenager she used to tell her two brothers that her love language was 'very big expensive gifts!', an outing or a hot chocolate and a chat were the things that made her feel most loved.

Personality styles

Although there is not room in this book to go into the detail of personality types, it is worth understanding that because of their personality strengths and sometimes weaknesses children are motivated in different ways.

Powerful children or 'lion' types tend to feel comfortable when they have a certain amount of control, while 'beaver' types, who are methodical and want everything to be ordered, need different ways of parenting. A lovely book that is well worth reading to your family, and which explains these personalities and the way they can cooperate in a family, is *The Treasure Tree* by John Trent and Gary Smalley. It tells the story of four animals, the lion, the otter, the beaver and the golden retriever, who go on a trip looking for treasure and end up discovering the treasure of each other's personalities.

Using animal characters, you can think of the characteristics of each animal and immediately picture some of the traits of the personality it represents. For example, a lion likes to be a leader, and a beaver is methodical. It is also useful to keep in mind the opposite traits. For instance a lion likes winning, therefore hates losing; a beaver likes order, and so hates chaos. These animal types not only describe how a person thinks and acts but also, with a little more insight, how they wish to be treated.

Understanding and accepting the personalities in your home can make a huge difference to the family atmosphere. It enables each person to be her- or himself, to respect and learn from each other's differences, and to work on strengthening areas of weakness.

Our parenting styles are often driven by our own personalities, so it can be an interesting exercise to try to understand both yourself and your daughter, and to develop a parenting style that works for you. If, for example, you are a 'beaver' type, who likes everything in order, you are likely to be the sort who says things like, 'I'll be with you in a minute, but I've just got to . . .' You will be a parent who has to tick off all the jobs on the list before having time for fun. An 'otter' parent, with a fun-loving personality, can find it hard to set and stick to boundaries; you never liked rules as a child, and even as an adult they can cramp your style. The 'retriever' personality requires harmony and needs to be liked, which can lead to the ultimate 'jellyfish' parenting style. And if your personality is more of the 'lion', then you are likely to be the 'Nike' parent — the 'Just do it' one — who lines up the troops and gives them the orders!

It is well worth aiming for a loving yet firm style of parenting, enjoying the different nuances in your family and parenting your daughter with your own and her personality in mind.

The friendship factor

It is true that a girl's identity and much of her happiness hang on the quality of her friendships. And it is through her friendships that she tends to have some of her corners rubbed off. She learns to make contracts with others and compromise for the greater good. The mini-betrayals and upsets of childhood set our ethics and help us decide what we value in others, but for many girls there can be painful lessons along the way. As one mother told me, 'It seems that friendships at the moment are the be all and the end all, and I am constantly talking to her about how we have friends if we are friendly, and trying to encourage her when things don't go smoothly. We also talk a lot about the things that upset her yet may not be meant to be cruel or hurtful . . . even if that is the way she feels . . . We explain how everyone sees and hears things differently.'

As we have seen, children are good observers but poor interpreters. They will take personally what was not meant to be personal, and only a loving adult can realign reality for them.

These are the years in which to help your daughter grow in friendship skills. You may need to facilitate opportunities for friendships by befriending the parents of your daughter's friends, and by suggesting positive acts of kindness and friendship. Not all girls will have myriad friends, but she is likely to be distressed if she does not have at least one.

If your daughter is the subject of some sort of relational aggression or bullying, then your first plan of action is to give her lots of love and support. Then, if it continues, you may have to equip her with ideas about how to assert herself and act on her own behalf. If the problem persists or is extreme you will need to intervene in some way, but be very sensitive about how you go about this. Confronting other parents very rarely works and can sometimes backfire. Begin with her teacher, and in a non-emotional way explain what you are observing and ask if she has noticed it in the classroom. Don't be tempted to go and sort out the other children. Not only is this likely to humiliate her, it will give everyone the message by megaphone that she is in trouble.

If you feel she needs some skills you could ask questions like: 'What did you try?'; 'How did it work?'; 'What could you do next time?'

Bullying can be very subtle with girls. One mother discovered her nine-year-old was taking money from home, and was distressed to think that her daughter was stealing. Concerned about this out-of-character incident, she took a step back and investigated more deeply. She discovered that her daughter was being bullied by a group of older girls, who were 'allowing her to watch them play' if she gave them something from her lunchbox or brought them some money.

Once she realised what was happening, the mother was very gentle with her daughter. She made sure her daughter paid back the money she had taken, by doing extra chores, but she also listened to her carefully. In this case she was able to say, 'Darling, you don't have to be friends with these girls.' This seemed to be enough to enable her to break free from the other girls' subtle control. Listen to your daughter so that you can offer adult wisdom and comfort.

> As we have seen, children are good observers but poor interpreters. They will take personally what was not meant to be personal, and only a loving adult can realign reality for them.

In our experience, where there are three girls, two will sometimes decide to exclude the third. What seems to be really painful for girls in this situation is that they can't work out what they have done to cause this to happen. When a friend turns against her at the instigation of a stronger personality she may feel a real sense of betrayal — it seems so unfair, so heartless.

As a parent, encourage your daughter. Explain that this isn't about her, but about other girls acting badly. Reaffirm that she is a good friend to other people, and that the way the other girls are acting is wrong. Try to divert her attention and energy into interests, hobbies and sport during this tough time. One parent told how her seven-year-old daughter cried herself to sleep for weeks after her best friend joined another clique. The mother decided to take things in hand, and set up an 'after school' calendar for herself and her daughter. She signed her daughter up for piano lessons and a drama class, and she added a library day on which she picked up her daughter and took her for a special 'date' at the library after school. The daughter became less distressed as she became involved in a pantomime with the drama class and made other friends. Within a few months the ex-'best friend' had decided that she wanted to learn the piano too.

A parent can help by asking a few questions and providing suggestions for a course of action: 'Think about someone else who may be more lonely than you, who maybe you could be friends with'; 'Even if you are not close friends, you can still be friendly.'

hot tip ✪

- The key to a girl becoming strong is to listen to her.
- When a child comes home and says 'No one likes me' or 'Everyone hates me', it can be hard to tell the difference between temporary exclusion and ongoing rejection. Ask teachers, friends and other parents how they observe your child interacting with peers or classmates.
- Provide a variety of opportunities for group activities. Sports, music clubs, Scouts and drama clubs all provide an alternative to school as a place where your child can make friends and gain acceptance.

Teaching her how to make friends

Remember that popularity isn't necessarily the same as friendship. Some children are quite happy with their own company, at least some of the time, and are content with just one or two good friends. Other children, by temperament and preference, feel the need to be in a 'best friendship' or group to be happy. However, all children need certain social competencies, and they will feel much more secure if they have some guidance.

As your daughter grows, you can privately coach her in great ways to build friendships. Give her ways to practise basic skills such as inviting a friend over or paying someone a compliment. Teach age-appropriate conversation openers and explain the rules for guests, such as 'You go first', or 'What shall we do now?' Teach your children how to encourage others in ways like praising teammates for a good game. Help them identify positive phrases like 'Great idea!' or 'Nice try!' Practise these within your family.

Making cards and gifts for friends or relatives also provide opportunities to practise these skills. Try to offer positive ideas that help your daughter take the focus off herself and put it on others.

Encourage friends from families whose parents you enjoy and who have similar values

Let your daughter invite a friend over to stay the night. She can make the phone call, but if you make an effort to get to know the parents you will help strengthen the friendship that is forming. It is worth the effort. Open communication between parents is part of the equation of building good friendships.

Getting along at school

School principals and teachers say they are often amazed that parents want to know how their children are doing academically, yet fail to ask the really important questions about how they are fitting in socially. They suggest the critical questions we need to ask are:

- Does my child have friends?
- Does she fit in happily?

Some children struggle with social interactions that just come naturally to others. These children need parents who make a conscious effort to encourage and coach them. Sue Blair, an Auckland mother of two, came up with 'The Friendship Game' as a way of equipping her five-year-old with the confidence to tackle her first days at school, and later, hopefully, life in general.

The Friendship Game

This was actually a series of 'what to do when' ideas, but Sue labelled them a game to keep it light and prevent her daughter feeling stressed. At the end of the day she could then casually enquire how the 'game' was going — or ask 'Which part of the Friendship Game did you play today?' — rather than embarking on an interrogation to find out whether her child was making friends.

Playing the game enabled her daughter to acknowledge that social skills might not be her strength, while giving her a plan for tackling the situation.

Action lab ➤➤

RULES OF THE 'FRIENDSHIP GAME'

➤➤ *Ask other children about themselves.*

➤➤ *Start talking before groups sit down.*

➤➤ *Ask a group if you may join in — don't wait to be asked. Join different groups.*

➤➤ *Be friends mostly with children in your class.*

➤➤ *If you must say 'No', say why and suggest another time. It's okay to say 'I'm not allowed'.*

How to play

➤➤ *Sit with at least one other person for morning tea or lunch — if you sit alone everyone will think that is what you want to do.*

➤➤ *Enjoy the games — don't complain or stop playing just because you are not winning or you are getting tired of it.*

➤➤ *Find out what someone is interested in, then ask them to tell you more about it (remember Morning News or other conversations).*

➤➤ *Have lots of friends and spend a little time with each of them.*

Helping your children grow in social competence

Most parents understand the importance of getting along with others and forming friendships, but they don't really know where to start in helping their children learn how to form these valuable relationships. We often expect our kids to pick up social graces from watching us, or to grow naturally into good social interactions. Unfortunately it is not always as easy as that. As with any other skill, most children have to be coached, allowed to practise, and encouraged to try again when things don't work out.

Encouraging good manners

Good manners have often been referred to as the base of the good-behaviour pyramid. Expecting good manners at home, modelling politeness, and using words such as 'please', 'thank you' and 'excuse me' should be family 'givens'. Teach a new manner each week, and practise table manners. One mother says she often serves food on large platters and allows the children to choose what they will eat, and they are expected to serve the person next to them first. Not only do the children eat a much wider variety of foods, but they also show a lot of respect for each other.

Social cues

Dr Lawrence Cohen, the author of *Playful Parenting* and several books on children and social acceptance, suggests that we can help our kids do better at reading social cues, which are often a challenge for children who have difficulty fitting in. He suggests looking through a magazine with them, or watching TV with the sound turned down, then asking your child what each person might be feeling. Follow this by asking them to make the same facial expressions. This sort of one-on-one coaching helps children to develop crucial non-verbal communication skills.

Staying close naturally

Dr Ross Campbell is the author of *How to Really Love Your Child*. He says that towards the end of the primary-school years parents, especially fathers, sometimes pull away, insecure about hugging or touching their daughters. But this is when you need to provide lots of affirmation so that your daughter enters the years of puberty with a healthy emotional bank balance. In other words she is secure in the knowledge of your total backing and can draw on that warmth and affirmation at any time. Whenever possible still hug and touch her, even if it is just a back pat or a shoulder squeeze. This age is when the final building blocks of conscience are being put in place, and your discussions provide an opportunity for her to talk things over as well as make a good case for something she believes in.

Confidence doesn't come from the curves you have

Nor does it come from the clothes you wear, or from the money in your bank account. Confidence comes from the messages you hear in your head. And the messages parents give to their girls will equip them with wisdom long after they have left home, ringing in their ears for the rest of their lives. Remember the ones your parents passed down, like 'Money is a good servant, but a bad master', 'A good laugh and a long sleep are the best cures in the doctor's book', or 'Worry often gives a small thing a big shadow.'

Milestones

Milestone traditions refer us back to the idea that we are growing up and maturing, and that the adults in our life are recognising that.

Establish a tradition in your family that on your daughter's 10th birthday you will take your her away, on her own, for a weekend with both parents. Allow her to look forward to it for several years, enjoying the expectation and planning what sort of weekend she would like to share with you — it could be a weekend at a beach, a camping trip, staying at a motel with a hot pool, or watching an equestrian event — whatever she is into. This will give you some lovely 'soft' time with your daughter before she heads into the more feisty years of teenage-hood.

The anticipation of this birthday treat is very important. She may change her ideas about it every few months, but that will be part of the deal and the fun for you all. When she is seven she may think she wants to go ice skating with you, and when she is nine her ideas may have morphed into a day at a funpark.

hot tip ✪

Keep your words positive. Remember that a parent's words are like light brightening up her day, or doing the opposite. Never label your daughter in a negative way: 'You're such a tomboy', 'You should have been a boy!' 'Why aren't you more like Jodie down the street?'

Practise using phrases like 'Can you come with me today to Milly's house?'; 'It's not the same without you', or 'Honey, I am so glad you are my daughter.'

Spirituality and your daughter

Humans are complex beings with a unique and special dignity. We have the ability to act with resourceful rationality and wise love. We can choose to show love and goodwill to others, and to care for animals and our environment. These abilities suggest that we are more than just the impersonal result of the survival of the fittest. Unlike other animals we are endowed with the ability to display character, to exercise courage and to live by our consciences. No discussion of traditions and milestones seems complete without referring to our spirituality. We need to acknowledge to our children that we are not only physical, mental and social beings but also spiritual beings.

Your daughter is likely to want to know about God and death and the other big questions of life. You must answer her questions as well as you know how. As Paul Vitz, professor of psychology at New York University, suggests in his book *Faith of the Fatherless*, in the future we may have to admit that one of the most serious forms of child abuse is when parents don't allow their children to develop their spirituality.

We live in a highly secular culture. And the Easter bunny, or Father Christmas with his red suit and huge bag of toys are poor substitutes for spirituality. Deep in our hearts we all know that we are more than a bag of chemicals, that there is something great about us as well as something flawed, and that along with human intimacy we need transcendence, a way of experiencing divine love, making sense of the world and our own flawed humanity. The rituals and traditions of religion and spirituality help to answer these questions in what is becoming an increasingly impersonal world.

If you have never explored these questions yourself, you can begin with your daughter and look for age-appropriate answers to her questions.

We need a community to help us raise our daughters, and one way to find that community is through the context of religion and/or spiritualty.

hot tip ✪

- ✪ Coach your daughter in friendships, but keep in mind that you and your daughter may have different temperaments when it comes to socialising.
- ✪ Prepare your child. You can tell her that she may lose a best friend at some point and it is not going to be her fault. If this happens reassure her that she is loved and valued. Acknowledge her feelings and comfort her.
- ✪ Discuss things that happen at school. Ask her, 'What do you think of what happened?' Increase her sense of mastery by discussing what she might do or say next time. Rehearse if necessary – you can even say things like, 'I'll be your teacher, you can practise what you want to say.'
- ✪ Keep a close watch on her use of technology and always be involved. Build trust in the way she uses the television set, computer, etc.
- ✪ Build her skills through getting her to choose one sport and one creative pursuit each year. Once she has made her choice, insist that she sticks at it for the year.

in summary

WHAT GIRLS NEED IN THEIR MIDDLE YEARS

Girls in their middle years need parents who:

- Build their confidence and encourage them to develop skills.
- Encourage creativity and initiative.
- Teach them values.
- Take the time to understand their daughter's personality.
- Coach them in friendships.
- Establish family traditions that give them a sense of who they are.
- Provide lots of affirmation.
- Allow them the experience of a spiritual tradition.

Chapter 9

Betwixt and between – the pre-adolescent years

If you lose your daughter between 12 and 13 you may lose her for later on ... about 14 ... you know, where girls really want to be with their mates ... As much as your daughter is a closed book, don't give up. Keep being involved – loving, communicating.

— **Rebecca,** *21*

Keep your boundaries in place – she needs someone to step up to the mark for her. At 12 you're really just a little girl still. Keep talking without nagging – even if your daughter appears to be blocking you.

— **Jess,** *19*

When I was 12 or 13 and started to get pimples my mother brought home a pack of cleanser and perfume and stuff. At the end of the day we all want to feel loved and those little things really mattered.

— **Emma,** *20*

I f you're the parent of a girl going through the 'tween' experience, you will recognise it as a period of constant change. These years are sometimes described as the 'Terrible T's' — terrific, turbulent, and trying.

There are wide developmental gaps between girls in the tween years. Even at the age of 10, best friends can suddenly find they have totally different levels of interest in clothes and boys. One girl may suddenly find boys enthralling, while another still thinks of them as just too weird for words and wants to keep playing with her Barbies.

The no man's land of 'tweenager-hood' can be confusing for both you and your daughter. Everything seems to be changing and it can seem as if your little girl — so natural, open and full of confidence — is disappearing. Fathers become aware of her developing body and don't know if they should still hug her. She seems to be distancing herself too.

The challenge for parents is to negotiate this time with grace and awareness. Your daughter needs you desperately, even if she doesn't give you that vibe. She will do much better in the years to come if she enters her teens with a healthy emotional bank balance, secure in the affirmation that she is lovely and capable. You are the adult, and if you can stay on your pedestal and still be the 'big person' when her emotions are all over the place, then you are offering the parenting she needs. Remember, your daughter probably understands herself even less than you do.

hot tip ✪

As Dr JoAnn Deak says in her book *Girls Will Be Girls*, 'Your tween will believe you have no wisdom, but keep acting like you do.

'Your daughter will pretend she isn't listening to a word you are saying, but keep talking, because she is.

'Call her a "tween" one day and when she asks why, lead into a discussion about negotiating the grey areas of tweendom.

'Play netball, jump rope, or jacks with her: help prolong the part of her that is a child.

'Tuck her in at night like she's a little girl, but treat her as a semi-adult during the day, especially when others are present.

'Try desperately hard not to embarrass her in public, but know you will be somewhat of a failure at this.'

Be proactive and keep her busy and attached rather than letting her flounder during these years. I love the teenage girl who told us how her dad had always done things with her, like teaching her water-sports and reading some of the books she was reading, and that he continued to initiate stuff with her over these years. She said it had made a big difference to her. 'When you are that age and your dad takes you out, maybe fishing or on a date, you can just be 12 and not have to be "cool". It takes the pressure off and protects you when you are going through all that other stuff.'

This is a great time to travel (see page 138 and 143). If you have a life goal as a family to travel, this could be a good time to fulfil it. It is also an important time to consolidate friendships with other families you trust and who share your values.

Friends

A best friend really matters at this age. As a parent, understand this need. If your daughter has had a break-up with a girlfriend, or some sort of distancing has occurred, be supportive as well as providing a shoulder to cry on. Back her as she re-establishes friendships, or do things with other families to fill a gap.

A group of families in our suburb who had children this age got together and ran what they called 'Whanau Fridays' for their pre-teens. Two couples took responsibility each week for organising activities for the group. Basically they created a great age-appropriate social life for their kids, and the effort really paid off later. What they had actually done was create a group of surrogate cousins and brothers and sisters for their young teens, and a positive group of friends for the coming years. Peer pressure can work very well when it is positive. Having a group of friends who mix socially, even if they don't attend the same school, really matters during high school. These families also found that the kids thrived in the knowledge that several other sets of parents really cared about them and later, as teenagers, they were aware of not wanting to let each other's parents down as well as their own. It is well worth making time for this sort of investment in your daughter's social life — the pay-offs are immense, and often include forging strong friendships for parents.

Whanau Fridays involved things like car rallies, ice-skating, video nights (always with great food) and sometimes discussions with older teenagers to whom the tweenies looked up. If your daughter belongs to a youth group or club, there may well be an opportunity for you to be involved in some way. Apart from issues of safety and supervision, girls of this age aren't as allergic to parents' involvement as teenagers are likely to be.

hot tip ✪

FOCUS ON AN INTEREST

Mary Pipher, the author of *Reviving Ophelia*, calls it an anchor — a girl needs an anchor that keeps her stable or serves as something to hold onto in the stormy seas of life. Encourage an interest or passion and take her to exhibitions, concerts or shows that will build on this focus.

The importance of staying connected during the 'tween' years

In their 2006 study of families where parents had positively passed on their faith to their children, the Barna Group noted the importance of the age 12 as a hinge point. During the 11 to 13 age range, most kids undergo huge changes and challenges relating to their self-image and their choices concerning morals, beliefs, relationships and life goals. This is often a difficult time in the relationship between parents and kids, but it is also a critical time in which parents need to make sure they stay connected and accessible to their kids.

Rites of passage

Formerly, most cultures had a ceremony of some type around puberty to mark a girl becoming a woman. It usually involved a rite, being surrounded by the older women, a welcoming into adulthood, and handing on of wisdom. In our Western, highly individualised society, if a girl has a positive experience of menarche — the time when her girl's body is transformed into that of a woman — it is usually actively orchestrated by her parents. Society as a whole doesn't tend to do it very well. A talk by the school nurse, sex education based on feelings and the use of condoms, and schoolground talk of getting 'the curse' can all be pretty traumatic for a young girl. Very often they just don't want to know — it all sounds pretty awful.

We suggest that forewarned is forearmed. If, as a loving parent, you give your daughter information couched in the social, emotional and identity contexts, as well as just the biological, she will handle the ups and downs much better. There is such a thing as 'imprinting', which is related to the way we first hear about sexuality. It is your privilege to communicate the experience of being a woman in the most positive way possible, giving your daughter a sense of her personal boundaries, potential and ideals for the future.

> If, as a loving parent, you give your daughter information couched in the social, emotional and identity contexts, as well as just the biological, she will handle the ups and downs much better.

Be her ally in preparing for puberty

Good information

Imagine knowing that when you get older certain things will happen to your body, but not being quite sure what these things are. Do you remember what you were thinking and feeling at this age?

As your daughter begins the process of becoming a young woman she will be collecting information from a variety of sources, and she may be hugely concerned about things you have not even thought of. Girls often become anxious about whether there is something wrong with them — her breasts seem to be developing unevenly, or she may think that she is becoming fat and ugly as her natural shape begins to fill out around the hips. (This is another tragedy of the 'thin culture' that surrounds girls — just as their womanly bodies are beginning to develop they are bombarded with unrealistic images of 'Photoshopped' bodies in magazines and on posters.)

Your daughter may experience unfamiliar pains and cramps, and she will need to be reassured that there is absolutely nothing to be afraid of. Make sure she knows she has all the resources she needs to cope, in terms of both her physical needs and your availability. Teach her that the changes she is experiencing are normal and that every girl in the world goes through these 'growing pains'.

She may be anxious that her friends have begun their periods and she hasn't. One of the most common fears young girls have is the fear of humiliation, that she may be caught unprepared at school or in company. She may have heard tales about girls 'flooding' or being smelly, and she needs to be reassured that neither of these things need happen.

Although many girls initially find the idea of discussing what is happening to their bodies awkward and embarrassing, it is worth pushing through that barrier to make sure your daughter understands what is going on and is prepared. A wise mum will make sure her daughter has good information about her body and the changes that will occur. When her breasts begin to develop, reassure her that she can expect her periods to begin soon after. It's a good idea to set her up with a feminine stash in a special drawer in the bathroom, and a small purse just in case she begins her menstrual cycle when she's away from home. Showing your daughter how to prepare for her first period before it occurs will alleviate many of her fears, and her apprehension about what to do when it happens.

> That awful awkward time when you are getting your period. You
> just don't want your parents to talk to you about that . . . You know,

your mother puts on that 'special voice'. I hated that talk. Bras and
stuff. I hated all that.

— **Jane,** *19*

A special weekend

One great idea is to take your daughter away on a special 'mother and
daughter' weekend for her 12th birthday. Make it something she looks
forward to, and plan what you will do together. Maybe take her to buy
her first lip-gloss or a new toilet bag. Perhaps allow her to have make-up
applied at a reputable store, by someone who is sensitive to her age and
will explain to her about how to care for her skin. Go to a movie together,
watch videos, sit on the beach, or plan an adventure like a canoe trip or
camping weekend.

We have prepared a set of two CDs called *The Big Weekend*, which
are designed to be listened to together in the car on a weekend such as
this (available from Parents Inc). They cover such topics as self-esteem,
romance, physical changes, hygiene, and all the other mysteries that come
with adolescence. The feedback we have had from parents has been
amazingly positive, and many mothers have said how much easier this has
made their discussions. While you are travelling you can listen to the CD,
then turn it off and discuss topics as they come up. If your daughter feels
embarrassed she doesn't have to make eye contact as you both have your
eyes on the road ahead.

Mothers say that this weekend has set the tone for a really positive entry
into their daughters' teenage years, and for lines of connection between
mother and daughter. If you have given your daughter the information she
needs in a positive way, she will feel much more empowered than if she
picks it up in compartmentalised snippets and without a context of values
or expectations.

A CELEBRATION DINNER FOR TURNING 13

A parent's perspective
When our eldest child, our beautiful daughter, turned 13, we

decided to take her out for a special dinner to celebrate. We booked at a nice restaurant where we knew we would be well treated, and organised a babysitter for her younger brothers.

During the evening, as we ate delicious, beautifully presented food and drank exotic non-alcoholic cocktails, we asked her about her plans and dreams about the future. We also shared our dreams for her life, and talked about relationships, work, men's and women's strengths, and our hope and prayer for the 'perfect' young man that she would one day marry and share her life with. We also gave her a small gift to commemorate the evening.

Apart from it being a special and memorable evening, perhaps the most significant thing was that clear, open, honest communication pathways were established as we welcomed her into the adult world.

In January our eldest son turns 13, and he's suddenly taken an interest in restaurant menus!

A daughter's perspective – two years on

I looked forward to it for weeks in advance, and when the day finally came, I spent a whole hour preparing myself for a night out at a classy restaurant. Mum and Dad told me they were taking me there as a treat now that I was old enough to act like an adult. Throughout the whole evening a special effort was made to make me feel grown-up, unique and loved. I was treated like a queen, with food and drink coming from all directions. At the end of the evening, Mum and Dad gave me a gorgeous little gold cross that I put on straight away.

It was an awesome evening and I loved every minute of it. Not just the food, but knowing that I was special and loved. It is a night that will be imprinted on my memory for ever. It's something I would like to do for my children, to show them that they mean more to me than anything in the world.

Birds, bees and body basics

Protecting girls from innocence and ignorance

Early-maturing girls need good information and understanding parents. Special challenges face young girls who, in spite of physically maturing bodies, still have nine- or 10-year-old minds. Talking to tweens gently but openly about more than body changes is a significant need, given the sociological backdrop most girls are faced with. The prevalence of the 'slut look', the push to have a boyfriend, and discos for primary-school children all combine to make this conversation critically important.

hot tip ✪

Doctors we have spoken to confirm that early puberty among girls tends to be driven by weight. Once a girl's weight hits 49 kg, puberty will kick in. Junk food tends to affect girls more than boys, as they store fat in their cells whereas boys tend to turn it into muscle. Boys tend to act out their emotional stress, whereas girls tend to store it in their body cells. So make sure you eat together as a family, and provide meals that include lots of vegetables and grains. As a family, use these years to enjoy exercise together such as bike-riding or hiking. Set some goals, such as how many and which tramps you will complete or hills you will climb this summer.

THE FIRST PERIOD

'As I was dashing out the door to a meeting one Monday evening, my 13-year-old daughter whispered to me that she had just got her first period. More hasty whisperings settled that she was okay and organised.

'The next morning I rose a little earlier than usual and put together a tasteful tray with two cups of tea, a card, a perfume sample and a gift-wrapped teddy bear. It was my way of saying,

> *"This is for the woman you are becoming", but the bear was for the girl that she still was.*
>
> *'She really appreciated the time taken to welcome her into womanhood. This simple gesture reaffirmed our mother/daughter relationship and reminded us both of how easy it is to communicate.'*

During menarche, not only the body but the limbic system (the centre of emotional development) is literally reorganising, growing and transforming itself in a very complex way. Your tween daughter is not a child anymore, but neither is she a teenager. As she deals with an array of new feelings and emotions driven by the hormonal onslaught of puberty, she may be alternately sweet, serious, crabby, distressed or defiant. Parents can be dazzled by a daughter who one minute thinks they are as 'dumb as doorknobs', but the next wants to be hugged and comforted.

These years are a mismatch between outer growth and inner maturity and wisdom. It is often a time of unexplained tears and emotional rollercoasters. It is a time when girls may become exceedingly modest, wanting to change behind a towel in the changing sheds, or in the dark at camp.

All this happens against a social landscape that is both risky and challenging. Because of the influence of the media, technology, peer culture and a changing society, there is some reason for parents to feel anxious. Tweens and young teenagers are dealing with more sophisticated issues than ever before, and often with less adult guidance. With 'mainstream' teenage magazines freely discussing such things as oral sex, AIDS and orgasms, there are few 10-year-olds who have not heard way more than their mothers at the same age.

Girls on the edge of adolescence are also targeted by a huge range of marketers who are trying to sell them everything from magazines and CDs to T-shirts and backpacks. And just at a time when girls' bodies are beginning to show natural curves and the healthy filling out that goes with

> Tweens and young teenagers are dealing with more sophisticated issues than ever before, and often with less adult guidance.

the onset of puberty, they are exposed to role models such as skinny supermodels who are severely below the norm for healthy body weight.

To a parent, the social pressure to be a 'hot chick' at 12 years of age is demeaning. You know that your daughter is clever, has a great heart and a great sense of humour, and you want more for her. However, conformity and camouflage tend to be the hallmarks of girls this age. Previously outspoken, confident girls often disappear, exchanging that childhood autonomy and invincibility for conformity and even an attitude of faking it if necessary, in order not to stand out or draw attention to themselves as different.

If having the currently fashionable clothing label really matters to her, perhaps you can do a deal whereby she does extra jobs and lives within her clothing budget by buying other items from op shops or chain stores. Teach her to sew and be adventurous in what she wears, within guidelines, so that she doesn't have to push the boundaries on modesty.

Parental angst can surround such issues as buying your daughter that stylish, yet scanty, top she wants. You know that it barely covers her anatomy, and is against your values, yet you recognise the need to balance your dismay against her anguish at being made a social pariah if she doesn't have the same as her friends. Fitting in is important to girls of this age, so try not to make your daughter feel different from her peers on unimportant issues. Keep your boundaries for the values and standards that really matter.

How to see your daughter through the middle (tween) years in a healthy yet safe way

Encourage play and fun as often and for as long as possible. During this time girls need freedom to enjoy lots of physical outdoor activities, along with continuing intellectual pursuits and the relaxed emotional environment of their family. Simple activities like playing cards or Scrabble as a family, or with younger cousins and friends, allow your daughter to hold onto her playful self.

hot tip ✪

- Family events, traditions and conversations are especially important at this time. They keep a sense of connection and continuity, and as she moves into the teenage years they are the best preventative components in keeping her free from drugs, school failure and pregnancy.

- This is a good time to travel with your daughter. It will give her experiences and family time before the natural pull-away from family during adolescence.

- Dads should continue the tradition of regularly 'dating' their daughters, and mums should instigate some special 'girly' times with her. Within reason let her choose the destination, and share her interest, whether it is horse-riding, a shopping trip, the ballet or a chick-flick.

- Delay any dating by your tweenager for as long as possible. Often girls this age become infatuated with movie stars or distant individuals, before they start relating to an actual boy. Many girls have maturing bodies without the emotional maturity and cognitive wisdom to manage real-boy attention. This 'virtual courting' is often part of the girl-talk pre-teens indulge in, and it is a safe way to show an interest in the opposite sex, without having to deal with a real relationship.

- Groups of girls and boys interacting around some kind of activity are the healthiest relationship mode for this age range – things like tramping, skiing, movies with discussions afterwards, ice-skating, car rallies (with parents, of course) and pizza parties.

in summary ✏️

WHAT 'TWEENAGERS' NEED

Girls in their pre-adolescent years need parents who:

- ✏️ Can still be the big person when their daughter's emotions are all over the place.
- ✏️ Keep her busy and attached; do things with her.
- ✏️ Understand that best friends really matter at this age.
- ✏️ Stay connected and accessible to her.
- ✏️ Make sure she has good information about the changes that are happening to her body, and teach her that they are normal.
- ✏️ Try not to make her feel different from her peers on unimportant matters.

Chapter 10

Teenage girls

Young women's brains do not fully develop until about 18 and young men's often not until their early twenties. We should not be treating the adolescent in the same way as we treat an adult.

— Dr Simon Rowley,
paediatrician and trustee of the Brainwave Trust

In the third form I was bullied the whole year. I was alone and isolated from all my friends and it was only my two amazing parents, who were just there 100 per cent of the way, encouraging me, that got me through. Home was a haven, a refuge — Mum's yummy afternoon teas . . . and she planned family nights on Fridays or invited family friends, just to let me be in a different environment. In the end things got so bad that they decided I could change schools the next year.

— Sienna, *19*

Self-esteem is derived from two sources; how a person views her performance in areas in which success is important to her (so if appearance is more important to a girl than academic success, gaining a few extra pounds may damage her self-esteem more than an F in maths) and how a person believes she is perceived by significant others, such as parent, teachers, or peers.

— Peggy Orenstein, Schoolgirls

More than anything, teenagers want respect from their parents. On the other side of puberty your daughter is likely to challenge your ideas and values to see if they stand up, but she also still needs your wisdom and experience, and you need to be very 'hands on' and available for a few years. As your daughter's brain matures she enters a different world, wanting to claim her independence and autonomy, and you need to facilitate this process in an age-appropriate way. It is as if you are moving from controller to coach, counsellor to confidant. If she knows that you are gradually handing over control to her she will not feel the need to break away in a negative way or through deliberate acts of defiance. But now that you don't have the control you had when she was a child, you have to work with the relationship. You become more an influencer than a controller.

Generally today's parents recognise that we live in a different and often stupid world for teenagers. Parents have been disempowered in many ways, and our society does not provide innate protection for girls. When things get tricky, and your daughter becomes rebellious or goes off the rails in some way, the system can turn out to be a blunt and often useless instrument for dealing with this.

Unfortunately, society gives your daughter permission to do much that you will not want her to do. In many ways, society is the Wild West for young girls. There are not enough sheriffs, and the old adage that it takes a village to raise a child has been turned on its head. You therefore need to ensure that there is a 'surrogate village' of loving adults who will work alongside you in caring about your daughter's character and safety. As parents you will also need to take an inventory of your own resources during these years.

> There is something wrong with a system that allows a 13-year-old girl to get contraception, get pregnant, get an abortion and come home and 'bleed out'. But under our Privacy Act the parents are not entitled to know about it . . . or that a child can run away from home at 14 but the police refuse to bring her home if they consider she is in a 'safe' place.
>
> — **Penny Lucas,** *youth worker*

So what are the resources you can muster to negotiate your daughter's teenage years?

Positive peer pressure

As we have discussed, your teenage daughter will be hugely sensitive to 'the group', especially in the early years of her adolescence. At times she will feel as if the whole world has a telescope focused down the wrong way on her, and she will need trusted friends and a group to whom she feels she belongs. If you can support that need in any way you are doing her a great service.

Having several different friendship groups is really important during these years. The people she meets through sport, an interest or youth group can fulfil her sense of belonging, so if one friendship group goes sour there will be somewhere else where she feels accepted. Encourage friends, preferably those whose parents you know and trust, and make them welcome when they are in your home. Be interested in their lives, invite them to stay over, and facilitate the occasional social event that includes their parents. Get to know the mothers of your daughter's friends. Sometimes they will be a safe person for your daughter to talk to, as you will be for her friends. Our daughter would occasionally bring a friend home, after some 'girl' crisis at school, and say something to Mary like, 'Can we talk something over with you, Mum?'

> My mum was a great role model. She'd get up early and take me for a walk. She looked after herself and exercised but was never, ever obsessed with those things or stuck on them.
>
> — **Kate,** *17*

More democracy

In chapter 7, 'Love and limits', we talked about Sylvia Rimm's 'V of love'. As your daughter matures, your ability to widen the V of love and offer more democracy in your home will give her a sense that you are working towards her taking responsibility for her own life.

As girls become adolescents their brains mature and they acquire the potential to think like an adult; what is called 'formal thinking', as opposed to the 'concrete thinking' of children. However, this process only becomes complete as young people bounce up against their parents and are pushed by adults to link choices with consequences. Your teenager will only give you permission to engage in this process if you have gained her trust.

For the last 13 years you have been teaching your daughter what to do and talking to her — now is the time to stop talking and start listening. You will want to know what she thinks and feels, and when particular situations arise you will need to ask her to tell you how she thinks she can handle it. For instance, how will she reassure you that she will be safe at a party, or what does she consider is a fair curfew? At the same time, you know that she is still part kid. She can be mature and responsible one minute and do something dumb the next. That is why you make sure she can practise decision-making on the unimportant things. Let her make decisions as long as they are not morally or physically threatening. She may have to come back and 'lick her wounds', or put what has happened down to experience, but it won't be life threatening if she dyes her hair, paints her bedroom a ghastly shade of pink or spends her whole clothing budget on one designer belt! She may simply be forced to learn to sew, or figure out how to get the best bargains at second-hand clothing shops.

Dr Simon Rowley from the Brainwave Trust puts a lot of adolescent behaviour down to brain growth. He explains that while the most crucial mental brain growth is during the first three years of life, a second growth spurt in the brain starts just before puberty. He describes the adolescent brain as being 'still under construction', and says adolescents are emotional rather than rational creatures.

Continue to make mealtimes a priority

Eating together as a family during adolescence has many lasting positive effects, not the least of which is the opportunity for healthy family discussion and debate, which Dr Rowley regards as essential exercise for the brain.

A University of Minnesota study also found that having family meals resulted in adults who ate more fruit, dark-green and orange vegetables and key nutrients, and drank less soft drink; that young women were more likely to eat breakfast, and both sexes put higher priority on structured meals and social eating. However, family meals fulfil many other functions during the teenage years. Healthy family debate and discussion moulds young minds and allows them to test ideas. Feelings can be listened to and processed, and perspectives challenged or affirmed. It is during these years that you can enjoy meaningful debates and discussions by both listening attentively and, when necessary, gently challenging your daughter's perspective.

Establish a tradition with your teenagers such as 'roast night', when everyone commits to being at home, friends are welcome, and perhaps you discuss a book or current affairs. For a few years we did something like this with our teenagers on Sundays, spending half an hour or so after Sunday lunch during the winter, sitting around reading a chapter of a book and then discussing it.

Action lab ➤➤

A DINNER TO MARK A MILESTONE

Some families have a dinner for their daughter when she turns 14, to which she can invite up to six mentors. These may be grandparents, family friends, aunts, godparents or any other significant people who have blessed her life. She prepares and delivers a speech in which she thanks them for their input into her life. Each of her mentors then presents her with a small gift, along with a piece of 'wisdom' that was handed down to them or that they have learnt to be life-defining.

This sort of family ritual gives your daughter the sense of community and belonging that she can use as an anchor while she creates her own identity in the years to come.

Teenagers and boundaries

While it's difficult these days to make teenagers do something, they can't make us do anything either. If a child is rude we owe them a roof over their head, meals, access to education, but we don't owe them anything else.

– **Diane Levy,** *family therapist*

149

Sometimes a daughter's moods and psychological power can undermine her parents' confidence. Remind yourself that you are still the adult and the payer of bills. It is your role, based in love, to protect your daughter. As she gets older each year she will gain more freedom, but in the meantime don't abdicate your responsibility, leaving her to a dangerous, unsupervised liberty.

Always be there for her, and hold firm to what you believe. 'We love you but we don't like the way you are behaving.' Put firm and clear boundaries around activities that could put her in a dangerous situation, and if she breaks your agreed verbal contract you may withdraw the parental help that is essential to all teenagers, such as transport, housekeeping and allowances.

Know who her friends are, and always stay strong, loving, fun and firm when friends who may experience an entirely different home life come around.

hot tip ✪

HAVE RULES ABOUT STAYING IN COMMUNICATION

- ✪ She is always to communicate with you if she moves from an agreed location to a new one.
- ✪ If she is delayed beyond the time initially agreed she is to call. She must always have enough credit on her prepay phone (the only kind a child should have!) to call you.
- ✪ Use texting positively. If she has an exam to sit or a difficult hurdle to negotiate, send text messages of support and love.

The vulnerable age: 14–16

At 14 a teenager tends to be at her most oppositional. She knows she can think for herself, and she can be quite dismissive of her parents. She is also struggling with a sense of identity and confidence.

150

As her life experience and maturity increase you will find that a different sense of self emerges in her final year of high school. In Stephanie Weaver's book *Teenage Girls Talk: 52 New Zealand Teenagers Talk About Their Lives*, 14-year-olds are seen to set great store by boyfriends, with romanticised ideas and the expectation that boyfriends will meet all their needs. However, by 16 or 17 the girls are becoming more realistic and empowered about their friendships with the opposite sex.

The 15-year-old daughter of a friend of ours wanted to have a party at her parents' house, and was humiliated by their refusal to allow alcohol. Her mother offered really nice food, a band if she wished, and non-alcoholic cocktails, but no alcohol. Her daughter insisted that everyone else served alcohol and that it would be the dumbest party ever. The mother calmly held her ground, and in the end her daughter chose not to have a party. Her mother accepted her decision, and said, 'Well, darling, that is your choice.'

Two years later, when she was 17, the daughter again asked if she could have a party at home, adding, 'And Mum and Dad, it's fine about the no-alcohol deal.' During those two years she had seen and heard about parties going sideways when alcohol was involved, had been to several where she had had a great time without drink, and had grown more confident among her peers about her own choices.

You may find that your 14- or 15-year-old will feel humiliated by not having a party with alcohol, but at 16 or 17 she may feel strong enough in her own skin to live with your standards and may even be choosing them as her own.

Curfews

Curfew times should not be hard and fast. Every situation creates its own 'be-home-by' time. Just be sure you have established that time, and that your daughter has the wherewithal to call if she can't make it by that time. Let her know that you trust her to communicate if she changes venue. You may think you are doing a good thing by requiring your daughter to always be the first one home out of her group of friends, but for her it may become an unnecessary and counterproductive source of embarrassment.

Love is being alert and involved

Let your child know: 'I love you enough to insist on a curfew, to discipline you if you have liquor on your breath, to chaperone your parties, and to take the time to be at your school athletics days, your musical presentations, and your academic events.'

Studies show that the main modifier of teenage behaviour is to avoid letting their parents down. It is particularly interesting to see that according to a new American study, laws that require minors to notify their parents or get the consent of one or both before having an abortion have reduced risky sexual behaviour among teens. Researchers Jonathan Klick and Thomas Stratmann found that gonorrhoea rates dropped by an average of 20 per cent for Hispanic girls and 12 per cent for white girls in states where parental notification laws were in effect.

A major US news network recently interviewed teenagers in a feature on the pervasive use of marijuana, and those interviewed said the same thing over and over: parents are the number-one anti-drug protection. Kids need someone to talk to and to listen to them — someone they trust. Other factors were sharing family mealtimes and having a faith. The value of church youth groups during the teenage years can be immense. They often provide a positive social life for teenagers, with music, humour, company, positive role models and mentors, and the chance to explore the idea of a belief in a God.

Establish a contract – verbal or otherwise

If your teenage daughter is asking for more responsibility and you are not sure she is ready, get her to write up some rules for how she will operate. For instance, maybe she is due to get her driver's licence and wants to use the family car. Have her draw up a set of rules that she will abide by when she uses the car. These may include making sure the petrol tank is topped up, remaining within the law by not taking friends in the car, and not driving on the motorway after 10pm. Contracts of this sort are a useful way for you to allow her to take on more responsibility while maintaining boundaries.

Don't nag her. If you need to communicate something and feel she is being turned off by too much dialogue, use notes. Sometimes a message on a Post-it note is a relief for a teenager who feels you are 'on her back' too much. Notes communicate in a different way, without nagging: 'Please bring in the washing'; 'Dog in need of a walk.'

hot tip ☺

- ☺ Let the small stuff go. Does it matter if she spent too much money on a gift?
- ☺ Some issues are too hot to handle if you choose to hash them out in the heat of the moment. Allow some cooling-off time – let your emotions settle and then discuss the issue.
- ☺ Look for ways of saying 'yes' as often as possible, especially on things that don't matter. 'Can I have a new outfit for the ball?' Negotiate or compromise. If it is possible to pay for half, you could both win.
- ☺ Continue to build trust through verbal agreements with her. Have a family password: a word she can use when she calls up from a friend's place or a party to let you know that she really wants you to come and pick her up without losing face. Let your daughter know you will always be there to rescue her.
- ☺ Ensure there are consequences when trust is broken, and that the relationship is restored afterwards.

The consequences of broken trust

If you need to discipline your daughter, then a useful principle can be CPR. We all know how to apply CPR in a medical emergency; the same

initials will help you negotiate a teenage daughter's misdemeanour —
consequences plus a **plan** plus **reconciliation**.

For instance, if your daughter as a learner driver takes her friends
in the car, the consequence may be denying her the use of the car for
a certain length of time, a weekend grounding, or whatever you feel is
appropriate. However, you then need to talk through with her a plan of
action, establishing what she will do and say if a similar occasion arises in
the future. It is then time to put the incident behind her and allow her to
carry on in a reconciled relationship with you. Remember always to make
it your daughter's problem, not yours.

> My parents always reaffirmed their love, even after some bad
> incident. They always talked about forgiveness and would say
> something like, 'We realise that you tripped up, but we believe in
> you and you are a better girl than this.'
>
> — Jessica, *19*

hot tip ✪

- ✪   Let the consequences do the teaching.
- ✪   Take out the anger.
- ✪   Stay on your daughter's side against the problem.
- ✪   Ask her for a plan to fix the issue.

Keep the problem in your daughter's court — don't rescue her from a learning opportunity

For instance, your daughter may be making a big fuss over the fact that she
has nothing to wear and somehow it is being portrayed as your problem.
There are plenty of clothes in her wardrobe and strewn around her room,
but what she means is that the particular top she wants to wear today is
unwashed and lying crumpled up on the floor. A lecture rises into your
throat, but instead you let the consequences teach, while you empathise
with her against the problem: 'That must be disappointing. You're right,

that cerise outfit would be perfect for today.' You dodge the accusation that somehow this is *your* fault. You know the problem, the cause of the problem, and the solution to the problem . . . but your aim is for her to do the problem solving herself: 'I wash most days. Can you think of a way of getting the clothes you need washed into the system?'

Coping with exclusion or rejection

> I was very different from the other girls in my class. I didn't really have a close friend during high school. Their values were different from mine, and I didn't want to be drawn into the stuff they were into. Mum encouraged me through hobbies and interests. She would reaffirm that I was a good friend to other people, and told me that even if I didn't have a close friend now, it would happen eventually.
>
> — **Natalie,** *19*

Girls can use exclusion and rejection, teasing and ridiculing as weapons. In some ways girls' bullying can be more cruel than boys'. One teenager described the first year or so at secondary school as the pinnacle of social cruelty, but said it got better towards the final years as the girls became more secure in their identities and popularity became less important. As one girl said, 'There are still the popular girls, but they aren't our leaders anymore.'

The cruelty of cattiness

Boys are aggressive — they fight. You can tell that by their cuts and bruises. However, what research reveals is that girls are just as aggressive as boys, but they tend to use *relational aggression* rather than their fists.

Passing on or texting nasty notes, revealing secrets, rolling eyes, sighing loudly or making mocking sounds when the 'target' speaks, and recruiting others to exclude the person are all tactics used by girls to label or exclude a particular girl. The power of relational aggression comes from the general perception held by girls, especially adolescent girls, that their worth and identity is defined by their friendships. Group affiliation is their number one value. To be ignored, excluded, not fit in, or be 'unchosen' is like not existing at all.

Often parents do not even know their daughter is being victimised. Girls tend not to tell their parents about bullying, because they are ashamed of their victim status, they believe their exclusion is in some way justified, and most of all because they fear their parents will do something that will wreck their chances of ever being readmitted to the clique.

And invariably, parents believe their child's side of the story, finding it inconceivable that their daughter could be a bully. Research shows, however, that bullying is very common: in one study 57 per cent of girls admitted teasing or gossiping in the previous month, and 23 per cent admitted bullying. Any girl could well be a victim *and* an aggressor. Rarely do girl bullies take responsibility for what they do — it's always the other girl's fault.

What can parents do?

It can be hugely painful to see your daughter as a victim of other girls' nastiness. So what can you do?

Take bullying seriously. By listening and empathising you will help her cope, and this may be enough to see her through. If a friend is involved in the behaviour, talk to her about considering honest confrontation. Coach your daughter to confront her friend about an offence rather than spreading gossip herself and reinforcing the cycle.

Explain that she may lose a best friend at some point, and it is not necessarily going to be her fault. There may not be anything she can do about it. Explain that 'not everyone likes everyone'. As Sharon Lamb, the author of *The Secret Lives of Girls*, suggests, 'Teaching girls to cope with someone they don't like, rather than reinforcing the nice-to-the-face/gossip-behind-the-back standard' is sometimes the most realistic option.

Inspire your daughter to be heroic. Research shows that other girls intervene between bullies and victims only about 15 per cent of the time, but when they do it is dramatically effective. It is amazingly healing for the victim, and can change the whole culture within a group.

However, the main thing is to continue to coach your daughter in friendship skills and help her learn how to genuinely affirm others, initiate contact and build a friendship. Continue to encourage friendships outside school if the possibilities within her year are severely limited.

Action lab ➤➤

TEACH HER ABOUT HEALTHY FRIENDSHIPS

Help your daughter evaluate what makes a good friend: 'How do you feel around this person?'; 'If you feel sad when you leave, and if you feel better for being around them, they are a good person to have in your life'; 'If someone constantly makes you feel awful, do you really want them as a friend?'

Romance, love and dating

Every woman longs to be fought for. She longs to be desired.

— John Eldredge, Wild at Heart

Man's love is of man's life a thing apart
'tis a woman's whole existence.

— Lord Byron, Don Juan

Modern relationships have become so complicated, with the separation of sex and love, that girls often confuse sexual attention with love. Her parents' respect, attention and real love will give her a plumbline against which to measure real love and respect, and show her what the counterfeit looks like.

I remember watching Michael Parkinson interviewing the comedian Dawn French. At one point he alluded to her teenage years and the fact that she was overweight. In her wonderfully vivacious way she responded, 'Oh yes, I remember an incident at the age of 15 when I was going to a dance on a Friday night and was determined to have sex for the first time.'

She also described how she was wearing red velvet hotpants. As she was about to leave, her dad asked if he could see her in his study. She thought, 'Oh here he goes, blah, blah, blah . . .' But in fact, what her father said to her was something that affected her decisions and her self-esteem, 'Dawn, I just want to tell you, we are so proud of you. Your mother and I love your conversation skills, your intelligent mind. Can I just say this. You deserve a really good man. Don't settle for some other girl's "hand me down" man.' Dawn continued, 'I went to that dance and no boy got to within 20 yards of me. They weren't good enough!'

She also went on to say that looking back, her father had been a real tower of strength for her. 'He taught me to value myself. He told me that I was uncommonly beautiful, and that I was the most precious thing in his life.'

For a girl the teenage years can be full of possibility. She has so much to look forward to, and if she has the benefit of supportive friendships and available parents the outlook can be superb. However, a girl's greatest strength can also be her Achilles heel. It is often in the area of friendships and wrong sexual choices that she suffers the most pain and anxiety.

Every woman yearns to be fought for, she longs to be desired. In Jane Austen's *Sense and Sensibility* Edward returns to pledge his undying love for Eleanor and every teenage girl's heart melts. Unfortunately, not many teenage boys understand this, and idealistic young girls often read far more into teenage romance than boys do. Help your daughter to value herself highly, enjoy lots of friendships with many peers in safe situations, and learn to value the character of her male friends before she considers serious dating.

Unfortunately, from a very early age your daughter may have been picking up messages from music videos and the general culture that adult or teenage life is about sex. The tragedy for this generation is the extent to which love and sex have become separated. Many young girls believe that sex is inevitable with a boyfriend, and that it will lead to commitment and intimacy. In fact, commitment and intimacy are so basic to a girl's nature that we need to teach her to expect those things to be in place before she offers herself sexually to another human being.

It may sound quaint and old-fashioned, but the commitment of marriage and a future together provide a girl with the ultimate security of man's true love. The life of a girl who has chosen to sleep with a boy at 15, has 'grown out of him' a year later, but has a child with him, and is therefore tied to him in some way for the rest of her life, shows how keeping personal boundaries intact offers a far less restricted life in the future. Sexual boundaries keep the door open to higher education, travel and myriad other possibilities, including a woman's good health. Early sexual activity is associated with a variety of sexual diseases as well as cervical cancer.

We found an observation a teenage mum made recently to be really revealing. She said, 'My parents didn't have any boundaries for us — they just expected us to have sex. I wish they had given me boundaries and dreams . . . Although I love my baby and wouldn't now be without her, I would have made completely different choices if they had expected me to not have sex with my then boyfriend.' Many girls tell us that they long for adults to give them permission to just be teenagers, and to affirm their belief that sex is only for marriage or a future committed relationship.

In 1994 the American Surgeon-General, C. Everett Koop, set out the best strategies for enhancing adolescent health: physical exercise, eating fruit and vegetables, avoiding toxins such as alcohol and tobacco, and delaying having sex until they are in permanent committed relationships.

Dr Nigel Dickson from the University of Otago comments that in New Zealand the pressure to be sexually active appears to be reinforced by adults, not by young people themselves. The very programmes that are meant to address health messages compound them because they deliver a climate of early sexual activity. As Dr Dickson says, at a time when parents complain that their children can't get out of bed on time, or keep their rooms tidy, we expect them to be able to negotiate the hazards of sexual activity.

There is something terribly wrong when in 'counselling sessions' 13-year-old girls are wringing their hands about whether they are satisfying their sexual partner or when 10-year-olds write to magazines reporting that they have lost their virginity and can't understand why he doesn't return her calls.

— **Michael Carr-Gregg,** The Princess Bitchface Syndrome

It has been said that a boy will only fight as hard as he has to in order to win a girl's affection. Without manipulation or game-playing, your daughter can set boundaries and standards that reflect her expectations of how she will be treated and her ideal for a future loving partnership.

Women also tend to want to be part of a shared adventure, and to share it with a man who values her and treats her as an equal. In the well-known movie *The Man from Snowy River*, most women love the scene where Jessica is rescued by Jim, her hero, and together they ride through the Australian wilderness to set up the ranch of their dreams.

It is not so much that she wants to *be* the adventurer, as that she is likely to want to be caught up in something greater than herself. We need to allow our daughters this ideal. A relationship is not an ideal in itself. It is only as rewarding as the quality of the character and dreams of the couple.

An email newsletter recently arrived in my inbox, and a portion of it is reprinted here as it makes a good case for protecting girls from the 'fall out' from the sexual revolution. What may have been manageable for university-educated feminists has not reproduced well in the lives of teenage girls.

GOOD IS NOT A BAD WORD

Eight years ago, a young writer named Wendy Shalit wrote what was considered a radical book called A Return to Modesty: Discovering the Lost Virtue. *While many people embraced the idea of a return to modesty — especially the young women whose struggles and aspirations Shalit wrote about — others were appalled. 'I knew that my arguments . . . might be challenged,'*

Shalit recalls now, 'but nothing prepared me for the tongue-lashings I would receive from my elders . . . [Feminist writer] Katha Pollitt called me a "twit" . . . The Nation solemnly foretold that I would "certainly be embarrassed" and regret my stance "in a few years".'

Well, it's now been a few years, and Wendy regrets nothing. On the contrary, she has a new book out, Girls Gone Mild: Young Women Reclaim Self-Respect and Find It's Not Bad to Be Good. As the title proclaims, Shalit is still convinced that true strength and happiness come not from deadening one's emotions and having sex for fun, but from practicing modesty and self-restraint.

And guess who's on her side?

As Shalit recounts, 'To find out why modesty is more appealing to younger people, [feminist writer Katha] Pollitt might have talked to her own daughter, Sophie, who . . . was disgusted by contemporary sexual norms.' Wendy interviewed Sophie, now a college freshman, and reports: 'Like many intelligent young women, Sophie Pollitt-Cohen now realizes that the boys' immaturity cannot be separated from the girls' willingness to provide sexual favors to those boys . . . Sophie rejects sexual exhibitionism even though she identifies herself as a feminist.'

Then there's Erica Jong, well-known novelist and advocate of what Shalit describes as 'the concept of a random, guilt-free sexual encounter between strangers'. Jong's now-grown daughter, Molly Jong-Fast, tried that lifestyle and found it utterly unsatisfying. The sad thing is, she tells Shalit, 'You're not allowed to admit that [promiscuity] just doesn't work.' Though devoted to her mother, Molly is 'embarrassed' by Erica's writings and says to Shalit, 'I was sold a bad bill of goods.' Well, their kids ought to know.

The sexual revolutionaries of the '60s and '70s may have thought they were helping kids avoid heartbreak by teaching *them to treat sex as a recreational activity. But those kids have discovered that was untrue. They've realized that the older feminists, who were supposed to be about women's rights and dignity, were actually advising them to make sex objects out of themselves! So they're fighting back.*

As Shalit studied trends like modest fashion shows and boycotts of sexually explicit T-shirts, she discovered that for every girl who's bought into the cultural myths about sexuality, there's another who is refusing to go along. While acknowledging the negative, anti-woman forces in this sex-obsessed culture, she focuses refreshingly on the women who choose to protect their own 'dignity' and 'vulnerability'.

From Chuck Colson's newsletter,
Prison Fellowship International, September 2007

hot tip ✪

- ✪ Be interested in her world: her friends, music, style. Get her to tell you about the musicians she listens to and the content of their songs. Talk about the messages the lyrics give. What seems harmless may contain negative messages, especially those demeaning to women.
- ✪ Stay in touch with her texting and computer habits. Go through her Facebook contacts every now and then with her.
- ✪ Coach your daughter in friendship skills. Few girls are able to distinguish popularity from friendship.
- ✪ Continue creating lots of opportunities for conversations. These are an acknowledgement of her growing maturity and a way of learning about her opinions and point of view.
- ✪ Don't allow yourself to be bullied. Girls who manipulate other girls also manipulate parents and teachers because it works!
- ✪ Listen to your teenager's dreams for relationships and ask about the views and values of her friends.

○ Continue to celebrate her great qualities and expect the best of her. She is likely to rise to your good expectations.

in summary ✐

WHAT TEENAGE GIRLS NEED

A teenage girl needs:

✐ Respect from her parents.

✐ Parents who are 'hands on' and available – she still needs your wisdom and experience.

✐ A 'surrogate village' of loving adults who care about her character and safety.

✐ Positive peer groups.

✐ Parents who listen to her – you need to know what she thinks and feels.

✐ Parents who talk to her.

✐ Practice at decision-making in areas that are not morally or physically threatening.

✐ To learn to value herself highly.

✐ To be able to set boundaries and standards that reflect her expectation of how she will be treated.

✐ Parents who are always there, providing support when she needs it, yet holding firm to what they believe.

Chapter 11

Raising girls on your own

If you can talk you can sing; if you can walk you can dance.

— **African proverb**

The more you are awake, alive and thinking and feeling deep in your own life, instead of zipping over its surface like a bug on a lake, the more you will have to give to your daughter and the more you will have to smile about as she grows up and you grow old.

— **Steve Biddulph,** Raising Babies

Earlier in this book, in the chapter on love and limits, we talked about really getting to know your daughter, getting 'behind her eyes', then developing your own parenting style. If you are raising your daughter on your own, this will be even more important. There are no rights and wrongs about what this might look like, and you can incorporate whatever works for you and your daughter, but there are some important principles. The balance of this chapter tends to be more towards women parenting on their own as they are more likely to be the primary carer, but many fathers are today raising children and rising to the challenge of balancing home and work.

A happy parent is a good parent

The first thing to remember is that your well-being is the key to your daughter's happiness. A happy parent is a good parent, and although the responsibilities of single parenthood may feel overwhelming at times, looking after yourself is a really important priority. You may not always live up to your own ideals as a parent, and you may take a slower route to get ahead in material terms, but try to enjoy the journey. And don't feel guilty if your daughter doesn't seem to have all the advantages and privileges of her peers. History offers us stories of many strong women who through hardship, and sometimes early deprivation and loss, have grown great character and become leaders.

Struggle is not a bad thing for children; a lot depends on how it is interpreted for them, and how small successes are celebrated. The interesting thing is that children tend to have a deep intuitive understanding of their circumstances, and they seem to understand their mother's lack of full-time accessibility if she is working to put food on the table.

Muster your resources

Between 1986 and 2001 the number of one-parent families increased by 53 per cent. If you are raising your daughter on your own, for whatever reason, a priority is to nurture strong relationships with other adults who are good sounding boards and who can encourage you and support you practically. Your daughter will need the community we talked about in earlier chapters, that of the wider family, friends and social activities. If you are a woman and have friends where dads are present in natural, everyday ways, your daughter will see a model of a man interacting with his family, his wife and other adult women. Sometimes girls who come from single-parent families have an idealised picture of what a husband–wife relationship is. They haven't seen the everyday cut and thrust, and the sorting out of conflict, and they may panic when they are in a relationship themselves and conflict arises. Seeing a husband and wife say sorry to each other, and observing a family handle a variety of scenarios, will allow her to create a realistic picture of the ups and downs of family life.

Children need to be fathered as well as mothered, and if Dad is absent they need to have a substitute, or some sort of compensating presence, in place. Many recent studies have found that the absence of a biological father, whether through death or divorce, causes a less severe crisis for children if a 'second father' — grandfather, uncle, mentor or stepfather — 'fathers' the child, in healthy ways, for at least a year.

If your daughter has contact with her father, try to keep your relationship with him and things like changeover arrangements free of acrimony. Although this can sometimes be hard, remember that you did do something good together in creating this beautiful girl, and your daughter will want to hold onto her version of her dad, even if it collides with reality. She is even likely to defend him if you are trying to get something from him on her behalf.

Firmer and softer

It has been said that if you are parenting on your own then you need to study the way an opposite-sex parent operates and incorporate that into your style. For instance, mothers sometimes need to become 'firmer in their softness', and fathers 'softer in their firmness'.

It is never easy trying to fill the role of the other parent as well as your own, but one of the vital skills is to master the art of remaining 'standing on your pedestal'. As you respect yourself, your children will respect you. You are performing the noblest task in our community — parenting — and you are worthy of respect from all. You may also rightly expect a measure of self-reliance and teamwork from your children as they grow.

One way to enhance the sense of teamwork in your family is to take the attitude, 'We'll get through this together.' It has been well said that, 'We have no choice about whether or not pain will come, but we can decide what to do when it arrives.' Children will catch a parent's sense of 'victimhood', bitterness or, alternatively, optimism. As you learn and grow and become the person you were meant to be, your children will 'catch' that attitude.

Routines are a great ally for single parents: they maximise cooperation. In the cooperative, fair and sharing environment that good routines create, there is also the opportunity to have a lot of fun and happiness. If you are a mother without a man in the house, you may have to remind yourself at times to remain firm and to keep clear rules and routines in place. If you are a father on your own, you may have to learn to be more nurturing. Listening, empathising and being emotionally available will mean so much to your daughter.

This snippet from Melbourne newspaper *The Age* (26 November 2006) offers a picture of a dad doing a sterling job of parenting girls on his own.

> *'Being a single father to Emily, now one, and Lauren, 13, meant that 44-year-old Nikolic had to learn skills such as painting fingernails, plaiting hair and shopping for bras and dresses — "all the girlie things". "For me raising boys is so much easier than girls," says Nikolic, who lives in Mt Coolum on the Sunshine Coast. "Girls have very different needs — it's the whole 'men are from Mars, women are from Venus' thing. But the girlie things are a parenting responsibility and it makes no difference whether Mum or Dad does them — I just go out and do what needs to be done."*
>
> *'The toughest time, he says, was when Lauren got her first period. "I was quite emotional for a few days — I'm a real softie," says Nikolic. "A couple of months prior to that we'd noticed mood swings at a certain time of the month and so when it happened, I was just there for her and helped her through it." Without parents or sisters, Nikolic relies on a tight-knit group of female friends whom he occasionally approaches for advice about bringing up his girls.*
>
> *'"When I'm dealing with Emily and Lauren, I try to think along the lines of a female," says Nikolic, "what helps is that we're so close and that I know them better than anyone."'*

Parenting teenagers on your own

If you are parenting teenage girls on your own, you will have the added weight of working through a lot of teenage issues without the support of another person. You are to be commended. Many parents who are going solo are doing a fantastic job, but it is hard. Again, wherever possible, make sure your daughter is exposed to good role models. As a mother, ensure that she has a male sports coach, a teacher, or perhaps has a regular meal with a family where there is a dad present. In this way she can join in family discussions and practise sharing her ideas with a 'safe' male.

When you are watching movies together comment on great men, and point out the qualities she might look for. If she is let down in some way by her father, try to interpret what is going on in a realistic way. If a delinquent father doesn't turn up for his access visit, or leaves his daughter on the doorstep having promised to take her somewhere special, don't tell her that Daddy loves you but he is being mean. There will be many mixed messages there. Say something like, 'Dad is making some bad choices at the moment . . . this isn't about you, darling, you are worth more than this.'

Girls from broken homes who have had their trust broken may find it harder to invest fully in future relationships. They tend to keep their 'anchors out', subconsciously holding back from fully committing emotionally in case they are let down. You can ameliorate her pain to some extent by building trusting relationships with other males, such as a grandfather, exposing her to good role models, and listening to her.

Create your own peaceful space where you can spend time alone. Let your big kids see that you take care of yourself. This helps them learn to respect you. If you work outside the home, why not build in 30 minutes for yourself when you first arrive home? Have an agreement with your teenagers that they leave you alone for that time — no demands, no questions or 'refereeing'. Then, in exchange, spend 30 minutes talking and listening to them. You'll all learn respect for one another's space.

Encourage your teenager's involvement in youth and sporting activities. She will then have other adult mentors to relate to and to give her the balance you may not be able to deliver.

hot tip ✪

Teenagers can put a lot of pressure on a parent for money. Establish an allowance for your daughter so that she knows it is her responsibility to manage her own budget and it is not an option to pester you for things. Be firm on this one.

So that she does not feel deprived, help her become resourceful so she can make the most of her budget. For instance, perhaps show her how she can buy one expensive piece of clothing or fashion item, then get other garments from op shops or chain stores.

Pursue your own dream and help your daughter pursue hers

By building a life that is satisfying and gives you a sense of competence and acceptance, you will enhance your own self-esteem. Pursue your own dream, whether it involves going back to tertiary training, changing careers, or saving for a special trip. It may take you a long time to achieve your goals, but hold onto your dreams.

Expectations and attitudes can make a big difference, both to you and to your daughter. Happy children are often those with appropriate expectations, who are grateful for small things. It is hard to underestimate the longing in a girl's heart to nurture something creative — it may be a great life-adventure, a social change, a garden or a talent. As a parent, you can model these things and enhance them through simple activities like trips to the library, or giving her a packet of seeds. In the words of the old saying, 'Wherever the heart is, the feet don't hesitate to go.'

hot tip ✪

- Remember that you are not Superwoman or Superman. Fix the fixable. Don't waste your energy on what you can't solve.

- Be your own best friend. Decide that your kids will look at a person who is strong and optimistic. If you need counselling, value yourself enough to get it.

- Keep some things private from your daughter – you don't have to share all your personal details with her. Avoid using her as a confidante over adult problems.

- If you are a dad living away from your daughter, remember that she will appreciate conversation and interest. Keep a diary, so that when you phone her you can show an informed interest in her life. Remember, men often talk only about facts, but feelings matter to women and girls.

- Be aware that you can say no to your daughter without damaging her.

- Join community groups, or perhaps a church where you can fit in and be accepted as a single, and your daughter can be part of an age-appropriate group. What is in your community – libraries you can visit with your child, children's clubs, women's groups?

- Pursue your own interests and set aside one night a week for yourself, whether it is to take a course, go to a book club or pursue a hobby. As the children get older, teach them a simple meal that they can cook on that day.

- Adult interaction is important for your growth and development. Going out with friends can make all the difference to the way you approach the next day. Attend a retreat weekend away once in a while for your own mental health.

in summary

WHAT SINGLE PARENTS NEED

Single parents need to:

- Look after their own well-being; it is the key to your daughter's happiness.
- Not feel guilty if your daughter doesn't have all the advantages of her peers.
- Nurture good relationships with other adults who can encourage and support you.
- Keep acrimony out of your relationship with your former partner.
- Master the art of 'standing on your own pedestal' – as you respect yourself, your children will respect you.
- Use routines to maximise cooperation.
- As a father, listen, empathise and be emotionally available to your daughter.
- Make sure your daughter has good role models of both sexes.
- Create a peaceful space where you can spend time alone.
- Pursue your own dream.

Chapter 12

Mothers and daughters

I remember when I was eight and the kids at school wanted me to kiss a boy. Being able to tell Mum somehow took away the embarrassment. Her hugs and reassurance made me cope. It's still just as hard the next day, but being listened to as a child, being able to get it out and get perspective, makes you able to cope.

— **Karen,** *20*

Share your views, values, faith in a fun, natural and everyday way. Write to her on special occasions or anytime with words of encouragement but also bits of inspiration. Communicate, communicate, encourage, encourage, communicate, communicate — be her safe haven — build up lots of 'emotional credit' ready to handle the 'tough times'.

— **Mother of a 17-year-old**

The thing that both my parents believed, especially my mum, was that I could do anything I wanted to do as long as I worked at it. I got my sense of being able to do things from my mum. She was a doer. Not a trained doer, a community doer. She just really believed that if something was worth doing you just got out there and did it.

— **Joan Kirner,** *former premier of Victoria, in Peter Thompson,*
Wisdom: the Hard-Won Gift

I was never in competition with my mum. She was always stoked for me . . . waiting outside school to take me to ballet, with a little bag of treats. She was great at building you up . . . You know, if you had a bad day Mum might instigate a fun girly time like going out for a coffee, or to buy a new lip-gloss. I especially remember her encouragement when I had to do something hard . . . you knew that she was 100 per cent behind you. If I had done something good there was often a wee gift and a note on my pillow saying how proud she was of me for doing the right thing.

— **Jess**, *20*

The mother–daughter connection

It's often the little things that we remember about our mothers — the normal, seemingly trivial stuff that connects us to them.

Mary remembers her mother as someone who would chat about the latest book she was reading, or a conversation she had had — often about dealing with life and faith — and she has rich memories from those discussions. The always-cheerful greeting and the smell of cooking when they came in the door; hearing her sing as she went about her chores; her kindness and love of family, her children and sisters, as well as for visitors and friends, are all etched in her daughters' memories. As children they used to complain about the fact that there were often 'unusual' or socially inept 'extras' around the dinner table or being entertained in the lounge. But their mother always said, 'You know everyone matters in God's sight, and the Bible says that we sometimes entertain angels without realising it.'

'Needless to say,' Mary recalls, 'as a child I had a strange view of angels as the misfits in life! But she taught us so much — through passing on wisdom and her faith, along with modelling a meaningful life. My parents regularly took night courses on a variety of subjects, were involved in community projects and their church, loved musical evenings, read to us at the dinner table, and instigated sometimes-spirited family discussions.

'A mother of five girls, she was often stretched by our different personalities and needs but she gave us a platform on which to explore the world. Her support of education, clubs, sport and making sure that we had opportunities to learn music, to take part in cultural and youth-group activities were often made with some sacrifice on her part. Her love of New Zealand native bush and knowledge of birdlife made picnics and hikes an adventure, and are all part of her heritage of memories for her daughters. The memories of rituals, customs and habits, and the tidbits of advice that come back to us over the years, are a tapestry we weave between the generations.'

Although our lives today are very different from those of our mothers, we must find a way of keeping the treasures handed down through generations of creative, strong women and passing them on to our daughters. We must build on the platforms that they built for us, and provide the platform in turn for them to function with integrity and strength.

When I asked a group of young women what was the most important thing a mother can do for her daughter, they all said, 'encouragement'. One girl commented, 'When you are growing up, you're so insecure and unsure of everything, from what someone said to you, to what you wear in the morning. You measure yourself against your friends all the time; their feedback is sort of what you think is true. But your mother can help you look beyond that. She stops you developing bad habits and encourages you to think beyond yourself.'

Another said, 'As girls you are always underrating yourselves and wondering if you are Okay. Mum would write me little encouraging notes saying that she was really proud of me — things like the way I helped my friend out.'

Another said, 'When your mother tells you that you are clever, beautiful or talented, you think, "Hey, Mum thinks I'm great," and it comes out in the way you hold yourself then that affects you in your life.'

And finally, another said, 'Her total involvement and interest . . . when you have to do your school speech, or helping out at sports day, helping with projects, going out for a shopping trip when you are down or have had a bad day.'

Great role models

Mothers not only nurture the character of their children, they nurture their souls. As a mother, you have the privilege of connecting your daughter to the wider community of women.

We need to expose our daughters to great mentors, other women who are inspirational, energetic and authentic. Your daughter will also need places to retreat to, and where she can talk over her life and her loves. Whether it is with grandmothers, aunties or female friends, her connections with women will always be a source of nourishment to her. Building a community of women whom she respects and trusts is a valuable gift you can give her.

hot tip ✪

Children pay more attention to same-sex adult models, and remember better what they do. However, girls are more willing to imitate male models than boys are to imitate female models.

Being a role model yourself

A friend of ours has raised two girls on her own from the time the youngest was three years old. She has had some really hard times to negotiate. Today she is the mother of two fine teenagers, considered the best babysitters in the neighbourhood, girls with character and resourcefulness. Both are at university and looking forward to challenging careers.

However, as a deserted wife, she says that when her girls were small she had to decide how she would face the future on her own. She says, 'It was my love for my daughters that got me through. I decided that I had a choice. Although I had not chosen this life for myself, I could choose my "attitude" and what I would model to them. I could model martyrdom and live with bitterness on a daily basis, or I could show my daughters something different. I decided that I would choose a path for myself, one that would be about learning and growing and becoming all that I could be, and hopefully that would show to my girls an attitude that would set them up for a healthy life.'

This mother offers us all a way of parenting. As we cultivate lives of meaning and worth ourselves, we model a sense of the future for our girls. Women are usually natural teachers of values and the interpreters of the emotional life that surrounds us. Those of us who are mothers must recognise this power and use it well. We are our daughters' first teachers and nurturers.

So decide how you want to parent and build in the 'magic' so that your link with your daughter grows strong. You want to help her build a life that incorporates ways to express her social, physical, mental and spiritual dimensions. In a world that for women often seems too busy, loud and intrusive, you will want to show her how to find moments of peace and pools of calm. Whether you have a ritual of hopping into bed in the morning and chatting about her joys, worries or problems; a spontaneous picnic in the garden, or an excursion to the beach, decide to be active in nurturing your friendship with your daughter.

Several years ago Mary wrote a small book entitled *Cappuccino Moments for Mothers*. In it she suggested that amid the everyday pressure of life we can lose the dream of staying close and enjoying our relationships with our children. In among the mundane caring, the ballet practices, doctors' visits, carpools and working we need to keep alive what really matters, and that is the fun times that become the memories and ultimately the connections mothers enjoy with their daughters.

time + understanding + enjoyment = feelings of love

Psychologists tell us that there is a formula for making sure our children feel loved. It is time + understanding + enjoyment = feelings of love. Just telling our children we love them is not enough, and when parents' schedules and external responsibilities become too much, children feel lonely and isolated.

Moments of connection don't have to be long or elaborate, they just have to be actively planned and instigated, even if it means that dishes are left in the sink and routines go out the door for the day. Mary suggests 'cappuccino moments' can be as simple as using the few minutes it would take to drink a coffee to plan a treasure hunt in the backyard, write a thoughtful letter of praise, or cut toast into special shapes for a cheer-up breakfast in bed.

hot tip ✪

Part of what makes raising a daughter so great an adventure for a mother is the potential for close friendship. In the meantime, though, your daughter is a little child needing your care.

✪ Try not to look to your daughter for your own emotional needs, or use her love and affirmation to top up your neediness. Yes, your daughter will be a source of great joy and love, but it is important to nurture your own adult friendships for support and self-esteem or, if you are in pain, to find help for yourself and make peace with your own past.

✪ Operate as the big person, the parent your daughter needs.

✪ Teach her what acceptable behaviour looks like. If your small daughter uses words to try to make you feel bad, don't take this personally. Saying, 'We don't talk like that; now run and do what I have asked,' can sometimes be enough. The important thing is to stay on your pedestal inside as a parent, be calm and loving, and operate proactively.

WHAT MAKES MUM THE GREATEST

Some kindergarten children were asked why they thought their mother was the greatest. This is what they said:

- *'Because she hugs me and she is soooo beautiful.'*
- *'Because she washes clothes for us and kisses me goodbye when I go to school.'*
- *'Because she played bingo with me last night and gave me medicine for my cold.'*
- *'Because she helps us do things. She makes food and calls us when it is dinnertime.'*
- *'Because she plays with me a lot.'*

Actively spend time with your daughter

Plan regular mother-and-daughter dates, and as she gets older enjoy together the feminine side of life — enjoying shopping or going to the ballet together, making cards for friends, or learning a skill like photography.

Support her interests and engage in something that you both enjoy, even if it is just shopping for special ingredients for a great dessert or cake that can become her 'speciality'. Let her make it when you have family or visitors for a meal and then enjoy the accolades and affirmation of being a great chef.

Read with her. Encourage her to read a wide range of books, especially books on courage and heroism, with role models who were known for standing up for what was right, who achieved excellence in their work and who showed humility and generosity in their character. Read her English 'set' books and discuss them with her. Watch movies together and discuss them afterwards.

More than one daughter

If you have more than one daughter it may be difficult to tune in on each one individually. Very often the second will choose a completely different route in life as part of establishing her identity, and they are likely to display totally different personalities. You may even feel more affinity personality-wise with one than the other; learning about the strengths and needs of your daughters' personalities will provide great insight (see 'Taking the time to understand your daughter' in chapter 8).

If you have more than one daughter, sometimes the cry 'It's not fair!' or the sibling rivalry is less about how many marshmallows there are in the hot chocolate than the subconscious plea, 'Do I matter? Am I important?' One mother who had two girls who were close in age set up a 'Mum's club' on a Monday afternoon. On alternate Mondays, after school, she spent an hour with one of her daughters in an activity of the girl's choice. The other daughter was required to entertain herself. During Mum's club the mother and daughter worked on activities they enjoyed doing together — perhaps a craft, making cards, creating albums, researching favourite topics on the internet, or whatever (within reason) the daughter suggested. Having this regular 'one on one' time with each daughter dissipated the demands for their mother's attention and the cries of 'It's not fair!'

Maintain your self-respect and values

During a discussion Mary was having with a group of teenage girls, one of the girls summed up what they had all been saying like this: 'I suppose deep in your heart everyone wants a mother who influences her — someone with wisdom and maturity that inspires you, and who you want to become like . . .'

So even if your teenage daughter gently mocks you and appears not to be listening, don't change your standards. Just make sure you have reasons for your beliefs and values. Equip your daughters with your wisdom. Sometimes family sayings or one-liners become part of the family 'lore'; sayings like 'Make sure your mind is a sieve and not a sponge', 'Be a leader not a follower', 'There is no problem that is so big that it can't be solved', 'There are always other choices', or one of my favourites (mentioned earlier), 'When something nice happens to somebody else be glad for them, not sad for yourself.' Let your words become a quilt of wisdom for your daughter.

Mothers and daughters usually understand each other deeply. They can have a closeness that is very beautiful — or they can form an explosive combination! There is often a time in early puberty when, even if you have been really close to your daughter, she pushes you away. As she deals with new feelings and emotions and attempts to establish her own identity she will need space in which to get her head together. She may spend long periods in her room, or have irrational outbursts.

Remember that she may not even understand herself at this time, and she is still a child with a lot of self-knowledge to acquire. Do not relax important boundaries, or family rituals like having meals together. But remember that you are the adult. You are far more able to stay calm and make choices about your own moods and behaviour than she may be at this time. After an explosive incident allow her some time out, then gather your own emotional resources, make her a warm drink, and go to her offering a statement such as, 'Hey, this isn't like you . . . what is really going on?'

Remember that your own self-respect is the key to others respecting you. So if your daughter treats you in a way that you would find unacceptable in others, do not reward that behaviour by continuing 'services', as well-known family therapist Diane Levy puts it. Not providing transport, money or laundry services until there is an apology should be your bottom line. Hopefully, however, your relationship need not deteriorate to this level.

As she grows, ask your daughter what she thinks is an appropriate consequence for betraying your trust or stepping over a line. She may be harder on herself than you would be.

hot tip ✪

TEACH YOUR DAUGHTER THE STRENGTHS OF BEING FEMALE

Show her how women can influence situations — change minds, master things. That sense of mastery may hinge on something as simple as getting her to change the light bulb herself and not waiting until Dad gets home.

Your daughter's view of men will be moulded by the way you respect and represent her father

Do not be her advocate with Dad. If he has said 'No' to something, don't go and negotiate on her behalf; send her back to negotiate herself. She needs to know how to make a good case to a man without using manipulation. Her father is the perfect person on whom to practise her powers of debate and persuasion.

Don't panic during adolescence

When your daughter, intent on forging her own identity, appears to push you away, want her own space, and question and even reject your values — don't panic. She is testing what you have taught her against values she has encountered in the wider world. She is likely to unravel the garment of values you have given her and reknit them in her own way. As long as you do not display hypocrisy between what you say and what you do, as she matures there is a fine chance that she will pick up those values again.

When she is being most critical of you it is often the time when she most needs you to be understanding — while at the same time angrily accusing you of 'not understanding anything'.

Protecting the special connection through the teenage years

As you both try to negotiate the unexpected feelings and mood changes that accompany puberty, it can be a shock to feel your relationship changing. As a daughter pulls away and begins to establish her own autonomy, a mother can feel sidelined and insecure.

There may be times when you have to call on all your inner reserves to be the parent she needs. It's as if she is trying to work through the contradictory feelings that you, as her mother, are odd, embarrassing and in need of help, yet at the same time the most stable and comforting person in the whole world, and someone whom she needs desperately.

Learn to read your daughter, while still keeping her accountable for her actions and expected to contribute to the family.

> *'The main thing I needed to know was that my mum was reliable. Because your teenage years are complicated, you need to know that you can trust your mother with problems and issues. Mum was brilliant because she was always available. We've never had set times when we chatted, but I knew if I needed to call, or talk late at night, or whatever, Mum would make time to listen.*
>
> *'That's another really important thing: listening. 'The better Mum listens, the more I'll tell her stuff . . . I like it when she*

listens; the sort of listening that's free from 'helpful comments', advice or solutions. It's especially good to know that even when she doesn't entirely agree with me, she's on my side. If she wasn't, I might just try to find acceptance somewhere else.

'I think the key thing about the relationship I have with my mum is that we have fun together. She doesn't nag or yell — and I try to be friendly and helpful. The hard thing to explain is that a lot of our fun comes from those 'in-jokes' that only we get. Like the accents we use (Coronation Street, southern, Aussie) or doing the dishes to loud music and making up silly dances. And definitely being able to laugh at each other.'

— Briar, 19

Address love and sexuality positively

It would probably be true to say that the deepest question felt by most people is 'Can I love, and will I be loved?' For girls this is an ongoing question, and her loves and friendships are likely to be to some extent your concerns over the next few years.

Focus on the big picture

As a mother, give your daughter a dream, self-respect and goals, and explain why sex outside committed love has the potential for more tears than joy. Explain that her personal boundaries and standards will give her the opportunity to fulfil all her dreams and enjoy quality relationships in the future. Let her see how she can enjoy friendship and even romance, exploring another's personality and getting to know them through doing things together and sharing lots of creative activities, without compromising sexual boundaries. Give her a dream of a future husband who displays character and commitment. Build on the information you have offered her in the tween years.

Action lab ➤➤

➤➤ *Explain that the guy she thinks is really cool at 15 might not have the same interests and passions as her at 25, and that if you have not had sex, it is much easier to move on from a relationship.*

➤➤ *Teach her what sexual attention looks like, as opposed to real friendship.*

➤➤ *Teach her that boys are aroused by sight whereas girls operate differently and need affection and closeness before they want to engage in intimacy.*

➤➤ *Teach her that the casual relationships that appear so great in Hollywood and on the screen don't usually work out so well in real life, and that with break-ups come heartbreak.*

➤➤ *Teach her about what real love looks like, as opposed to the culture of casual oral sex and impersonal liaisons, and that a guy will only work as hard as he has to to win a girl. As one teenage girl put it, 'You know, we had oral sex at a party and the guy didn't even look at me. I felt like nothing. I can't believe that I let him do that.'*

➤➤ *Encourage group activities, including mixed youth-group and family-group activities as much as possible.*

Faithful relationships are based on more than just feelings: actions and commitment are needed. Explain to your daughter how lifelong partnerships are based on building a life together, full of shared interests, projects and values. You may not be able to communicate all these messages to your daughter directly, but by setting age-appropriate rules for her, valuing her highly and having high expectations for her future, you are giving her the best chance of choosing a great future partner. (*Sex with Attitude*, available from Parents Inc, deals with boundaries and is a great resource for teenagers.)

Grooming, grace and poise

What a girl does with her looks through grooming, grace and poise says far more than any stunning natural attributes.

If necessary, address your own self-esteem issues, and facilitate your daughter's feelings of acceptance through what she wears. Children are emotional chameleons. If a mother lacks confidence in her own attractiveness and femininity, and expresses this through dressing down and being careless about her appearance, it will have an impact on her daughter. She might follow your lead, be embarrassed in public, or rebel against it. Be sensitive to her need to feel accepted, while balancing the reality of budgets and teaching her resourcefulness.

Girls without dads have less of an idea than others of how their clothes (or lack of them!) affect guys. Make sure your daughter has a full-length mirror.

hot tip ✪

- ✪ Be a great listener. Create safe times when she can talk to you, like cuddling up in bed in the morning, when she first comes home from school, or mother-and-daughter dates.

- ✪ Set up rituals and fun times of connection, which will provide happy memories and build love.

- ✪ Celebrate special milestones, like turning 13 or getting her first period. Commission some professional photographs of significant events, like starting school, etc.

- ✪ Spend exclusive time with your daughter, giving her your undivided attention. Chat while doing dishes together. Go out together for coffee or fruit juice, or even a walk in the park with a thermos flask – she will enjoy it as a 'grown-up' outing. The important thing is to spend relaxed time together.

- ✪ Learn to give her space during the 'prickly' patches. Be aware also that sometimes she will be having to deal with the cattiness and cruel conspiracies of her school-girl culture.

- ✪ Monitor your own speech – how often does your daughter hear you talking about diets and dissatisfaction with your weight? Model fun and celebration with food.

- ✪ Model and facilitate friendships. Befriend your daughter's friends, make them welcome in your home, get to know their parents, and show your daughter how to nurture a friendship. Suggest positive acts of kindness and friendship.

❁ Give her good information about her body and the physical changes that are taking place, and show her the 'great value' she has in your eyes.

❁ Don't compromise your standards. They will be a beacon of stability during the storms of adolescence, and into the future.

❁ Don't enable teenage sex. Let her know your boundaries, and that your need to know where she is and who she is with are based on the great value she has to you.

❁ Expose her to heroines. Point to powerful, wonderful women.

❁ Be specific. Name the actions, accomplishments and values of women you admire. Give her books about women in maths, science and history, and model choices for women.

❁ Keep your daughter connected to the family by giving her responsibilities, such as caring for the dog, cooking a meal once a week, or packing and unpacking the dishwasher. Every teenager needs to feel they are part of the team, and that with growing maturity comes more democracy but also more responsibility.

in summary

WHAT DAUGHTERS NEED FROM MOTHERS

A daughter needs a mother who will:

➥ Encourage her.

➥ Expose her to great mentors, and build a community of women she respects and trusts.

➥ Be a positive role model.

➥ Maintain her own self-respect and values.

➥ Keep alive the fun times.

➥ Teach her about healthy friendships.

➥ Give her a dream, self-respect and goals.

Chapter 13

Dads and daughters

He had a sense of fun. He was always interested in my life — did my projects with me and turned them into a fun father/daughter time. It was sort of teamwork — lots of support. He even made a walk along the beach fun.

— **Sarah,** *18*

He always took my opinions really seriously. He made eye contact and always made me feel so valuable — even in front of his friends. He gave me a thirst for knowledge.

— **Rebecca,** *20*

At about 12 when everything is changing and you're feeling a bit confused — there's lumps and bumps where you've never had them before — I remember Dad sort of metaphorically scooping me under his wing. He asked me if I would like to start running with him. It was so cool, and our time together. We did a half-marathon together as a little project. It has been a huge thing in my life that both my parents affirmed the idea of beautiful from the inside out. In our form there were so many girls with anorexia, not eating and stressing over boyfriends.

— **Jess,** *19*

There's an amazing gift a dad can give his daughter. Of course, she wouldn't turn her nose up at a new Toyota Corolla, or a wad of cash — and I wish I could give my daughter those things — but any dad can give her something far more valuable: a sense of self, a confidence in her femininity, and an awareness of her competence and potential.

Both mums and dads can load really powerful messages into their daughters' hearts, setting them up for a great life of healthy relationships and achievement. To be a dad to a daughter is a big responsibility. People talk about being a great dad — to be perfectly honest, most of us are just good dads.

The father-daughter connection is unique. You are the first man she ever gave her heart to, and that will never change. The relationship you offer her provides protection and approval, and it gives you a privileged position in her life, a unique opportunity to speak to her emerging identity.

You don't have to be a perfect or brilliant dad to give your daughter a great start. There is room for imperfections and mistakes.

Your daughter will appreciate knowing, however, if you think she is special. It has been suggested that at puberty the source of a girl's self-esteem transfers from her mother to her father. During these years she seems to rely much more heavily on what her father thinks, and on his approval. Your daughter must feel the enveloping security of your physical and emotional arms. You must always affirm her person rather than her performance.

My 'favourite' daughter, Kim (I always called her my favourite daughter when she was little, but she was smart enough to know she was also my 'only' daughter), was sandwiched between two boisterous, competitive brothers. I admire the way she held her own, standing up for herself, adroitly stepping around their muscle and brawn. Always choosing her own path, sometimes she was amazingly feminine against the backdrop of testosterone and noise, at other times totally a match even for that. She was also fiercely loyal to her brothers; the younger one remembers being defended by his big sister in the playground, recalling how 'with hair flying like William Wallace in *Braveheart*, she jumped off the monkey bars and dared the young offender to touch her brother again!'

My maleness resonated with my sons, and we instantly connected over 'blokey' things like sport and tools. But for me Kim was a bit more of a mystery to me . . . just like her mother. And, just as with Mary, my relationship with Kim was not based on our similarities but on a very natural, healthy appreciation and respect for her as 'something different', a female.

Most of my parenting in those days was by trial and error, but it came out of something deep inside me that was fiercely protective and, I now realise, in response to the unspoken questions asked by every little girl: 'Am I lovely? Am I acceptable and capable?'

Very early on, I got the strong impression that a dad does have an important role. My daughter looked to her mum to see how to become a woman, but she was looking to me for affirmation and approval. As a dad, I had the luxury of not being the main caregiver. I was the one who would surprise the kids by bringing home milkshakes, and initiating the after-dinner races and the rough-and-tumble games. I would allow her, as a toddler, to win at least some of the races, and would arbitrate creatively when she felt overwhelmed by her competitive brothers. I suppose now I wish that, as a young dad, I had taken more time just to delight in her. However, I am grateful to her for her forgiveness of those things I got wrong and for the fact that her memories tend to be largely positive.

Yes, you're lovely

For too many years men have considered the raising of a daughter her mother's job. Fortunately, today's fathers are clicking on to the important role men play in a girl's experience and view of herself.

Your words will be like beacons during times of self-doubt, and your belief in her will be like reinforcing steel in a concrete column. When life's earthquakes happen she won't crumble because that inner strength will give her the confidence to know that life's hard times pass and when they are over the lessons learnt will be character building.

She needs to hear from you, her father, in a thousand different ways,

'Yes, you're lovely, capable and clever.' It doesn't matter whether I am speaking at a parenting seminar, a corporate meeting or 'on air', the response is always the same; women always share their heartfelt longing to have heard those words from their fathers. When we speak with successful women, it is amazing how often they credit their fathers with using empowering words about them during their childhood and adolescence. A father can coach a girl towards independence and give her practical skills that will equip her for life in a unique way.

Your daughter needs your affirming words even at times when there is no direct connection between her behaviour and your loving support. In fact, it is not unlikely that she needs your support most when she is acting the worst. Your affirmation needs to be about her as a person, not her performance.

She also needs your strength. In speaking to a mother whose daughter became really rebellious during her teenage years, I was amazed at her conclusion that a consistent thread through the lives of all the girls who got into trouble at this stage was that they all had fathers who were passive. Many were just good Kiwi men, who wanted to be their daughter's friend and weren't prepared to get involved in setting boundaries, consequences, and expectations for their daughters. Although it was only an observation, this mother said it seemed as if the girls had something inside them that made them test their fathers to see if they would fight for them.

DADS AND DAUGHTERS

He takes us fishing and four-wheel driving. He fixes me when I hurt myself. **Shauna,** *7, Glenfield*

He helps me skip. He chases me. He jumps on the trampoline. Sometimes he takes me to the rugby and he takes me for swims and I love him to bits. **Lucy,** *6, Sandringham*

He gives me hugs and kisses and helps me with my homework. He takes me to get ice cream and he can fix things if they break.

Alexandra, *6, Pakuranga*

He is one of those dads you can't buy at the shop. He makes the dinner and feeds our cat.　　　　**Carla,** *11, Pakuranga*

He built our house and our playhouse. For me he is the best dad around. He can be a bit bossy but I really don't mind.

Naomi, *9, Waiuku*

He's smart, funny, caring, thoughtful and different to all other dads.

Chye-Xian, *9, Glenfield*

He goes in the pool with me, he looks after our family and he knows a lot about computers.　　　　**Emma,** *6, Waiuku*

My stepdad is a bodybuilder and can lift heavy things. He takes me to school and to dancing. He is the best banana cake baker. He lets me beat him at chess. Even though he is hairy, he's a good surfer.　　　　**Hannah,** *9, Mairangi Bay*

Jo Malcolm — *Kiwi Dads : A Celebration of New Zealand Heroes*

Be her hero

Your daughter's need for emotional protection is as important as her need for physical protection. And this special place of trust you hold as a dad needs to be handled with a sense of privilege. You can offer solid boundaries to instruct and protect your daughter, and you can be the hero who responds when she is in distress. She needs to know that if she is in any sort of trouble you are there for her. She needs to know that when you set boundaries they are for her safety, and because of your love for her.

A friend recounted how he had always told his daughter that wherever she was, she could always contact him if she was in any sort of trouble. One night when she was 16 she was at a party; her parents knew where it was and who she was with, and they were not expecting her home for some time. Then at 10pm they received a phone call that went something like this: 'Dad . . . Hey, that's not fair, I've only been here a little while . . . Okay, okay . . . Do you know where to come? 24A . . . All right, two toots . . .' During the course of the conversation the father realised that his daughter wanted to get out of there and was using the phone call as a ruse, so as not to lose face; something was going on and she needed to leave the party. My friend said, 'I drove there like James Bond. I tooted twice and my daughter rushed out and jumped into the car. She sat down with a sigh and said, "Oh Dad — thanks soooo much. The party was going to custard, I didn't feel safe and the only thing I could think of was to get you here."'

Balance age-appropriate safety and independence

Don't be tempted to overprotect her

A father is instrumental in developing competence and self-reliance, so you will introduce her to the wider, wilder world, enabling her to gain confidence as she grows.

What you want for your daughter is someone who can stand tall and know that she has the skills to handle life's challenges. She also needs to know where to go when she needs more resources. You want her to think for herself, persist, and say 'no' when necessary. Encourage her to think things through and to trust her own judgement.

You want her to have a go, not always wait for someone else to do it, whether it is changing a light bulb, unblocking a sink or putting the chain back on her bike. Of course, there will be times when she will be very happy for her dad to fix her bike, but you need to show her how impressed you are when she makes things happen or solves a problem herself.

> ## hot tip ✪
>
> ✪ A great principle for fathers to use when teaching their daughters is: 'You watch me, you help me, I'll help you, I'll watch you.'
>
> ✪ The best thing you can do for your daughter is give her the resources to face the world; don't overprotect her or hide her from the world.

This world holds dangers for our daughters, but overprotection doesn't work, and it tells your daughter that you don't trust her. Instead, wherever possible work with other parents to make the world a better place for girls. Demand an end to violence against females, media sexualisation of girls, pornography, and 'boys are better than girls' attitudes.

Get her playing sports and being physically active

The most physically active girls have fathers who are active with them. Start young, and play ball games, tag, jump rope, basketball, hockey, soccer, or just take walks . . . you name it! Physically active girls are less likely to get pregnant, drop out of school or put up with abuse.

How you value her is important

A father's evaluation of his daughter's worth and beauty, whether it is spoken or unspoken, has a huge bearing on her sense of self. When a father affirms, hugs and encourages his daughter for who she is — loving every aspect of her 'just the way she is' — he is helping her to avoid the slippery paths of self-doubt and false evaluation from the outside world.

A recent Auckland study linked a high percentage of girls who develop eating disorders with fathers who think that beauty is related to thinness. By all means, model and teach healthy attitudes to food, but never criticise, or even comment on, her weight. You certainly can engage your daughter as your personal coach, and get her to come jogging with you, but make sure it is about you needing to regain some fitness, not about *her* weight.

A father's encouragement and support can turn a negative event into a 'step up', rather than a life-defining disability. In her book *How Jane Won*, Sylvia Rimm tells the story of Mary Taylor, who grew up in China as the daughter of missionary parents. As a young girl during World War II she spent three years in a Japanese concentration camp, and she related how her parents' inspiring words were a guiding light during that dark time. After the war she returned to the US, where at the age of 14 she lost her left hand in an accident. Again it was her parents' words that gave her the platform not to see herself as 'handicapped', but as someone with a life full of possibilities:

'My dad's words have been like a banner, written across my sky for more than 40 years,' she said. 'My dad believed in me. He said, "Handicaps have nothing to do with the outside of a person. Handicaps are only on the inside of a person." He said his Mary had no handicaps on the inside. He encouraged me to read Helen Keller, do a project on Roosevelt, and showed me that inspiring others has nothing to do with what physical limitations we have. My dad refused to let me sink into the world of "I can't". He pulled me into the world of "I can". My dad's believing in me was a defining moment. My mother also refused to allow me to play "pity me" when I lost my hand. I went to college and graduated magna cum laude. I majored in speech and starred in intercollegiate debating. Today I tie my shoes, make quilts, hang wallpaper, drive a car and work on the computer.'

Treat her with respect and courtesy, and make this a better world for girls

When a dad acts with respect and courtesy around his daughter, it sets the standard. She knows how she should be treated and is less likely to fall for a partner who doesn't offer her similar respect. If you respect your daughter (and her mother) then she will insist on other males doing the same. If you put her down, she may allow other males to do so too, thinking this is normal.

While it's great to see many women hitting the heights careerwise, I still despair at the sight of too many girls setting their sights so low. They sell themselves short, and settle for abusive relationships with no-hopers and dead-end jobs. Long before they run out of talent and potential, they run out of vision.

> When I was little Dad used to give me 'butterfly kisses' and then as I got older big hugs. To have that obvious affection meant that I didn't need to go looking for it anywhere else.
>
> — **Olivia,** *17*

Get involved in your daughter's activities, and support her in special projects. Make time for one-on-one excursions and events. By doing this you are building opportunities for her to test her ideas against a man and to practise debate and discussion. By driving her friends to sport, coaching a team, or simply being a polite host to her friends, you are emulating a good male role model and helping to make the world better for girls.

> Father/daughter time is really important, e.g. driving to school in the car, special 'dates' and adventures — Jess remembers sleeping overnight on our runabout with her dad, catching fish and cooking breakfast on a beach for her Brownie 'survivor' badge (she also remembered that I had packed a 'survival kit'!).
>
> — **Jennie,** *mother of an 18-year-old*

Never too tough – never too tender

A father builds solid boundaries to instruct and protect his daughter, but he also plays wild, exciting games and teaches her to take smart risks. As one girl said, 'I know my mother loves me, but my father excites me.' Think of it. He is the first one to throw her in the air as a baby, the first one to give her horsey rides or to jump her over the high waves. It is his strong arms and reassurance that teach her it is okay and can be fun.

Paul Vitz, a professor of psychology at New York University, makes some interesting observations in an article entitled 'The Father Almighty,

Maker of Male and Female' (on www.paulvitz.com):

'In a developmental sense, each child, male or female, has two major tasks in front of them. Psychologists refer to one of these tasks as individuation. This is the process of separating oneself from others, especially from the mother or mother figure. For a variety of reasons, male children find this task easier than female children. In part, it is because both the mother and the baby boy recognize the boy as different, and therefore separation and autonomy come more easily to the boy. A contributing factor is that male children are relatively less interested in people and in relationships, and more interested in objects and spatial exploration than female children. As a result psychologists generally agree that autonomy and independence come more easily to boys than to girls.

'For the daughter, who is similar to the mother and closely tied to her, individuation can often be a problem . . . One of the important natural functions of the father is to help his daughter separate from the mother, to help the daughter form her own identity, and to keep her from remaining 'merged' with her mother.

'The other major task for both sexes is the development of sexual or gender identity. This task is reliably understood by psychologists as more difficult for males than females . . . from the beginning, and apparently in all societies, little girls see in their mother the meaning of womanhood every day in very concrete ways, and understand this as basic to their identity. They have an adult woman close by to model the meaning of femaleness for them. What fathers do [as] fathers is far less obvious.

'A good father enhances the sexual identity of his own daughters. Much research has shown that girls raised without fathers tend to be less sure of their lovability and femininity. As a result, they are more vulnerable to pathologies ranging from depression to promiscuity.'

Be the rock of Gibraltar

The best advice I have ever come across — and I humbly relay it to the current generation of fathers — is to be the most affirming and tender dad ever, balanced with firm enforcement of rules and boundaries. Think 'rock of Gibraltar' — fun and pleasant, but solid and safe.

Sometimes we dads need to take a raincheck and ask ourselves, 'Am I fun to live with — or am I becoming a boring old buzzard?'

Listen to your daughter – no conversation means no interest

Be interested in what your daughter thinks, believes, feels, dreams and does. Your daughter, like all women, is wired for relationships. Learn to ask questions, and follow through with conversations. One of my favourite conversation starters with the women in my life is, 'Tell me about two things that happened today and how you feel about them.'

Let her practise conversation on you. Talking in the car or during a walk or a bike ride are all ways to chat with your daughter. She will be able to handle her stress much better when she has someone to talk to. We men tend to be verbally challenged, but you don't need to do much of the talking. Just listen and say things like, 'Mmmm', or 'Anything else?' This may be all she needs. Women and girls tend to solve their problems by talking about them, so don't feel you need to rescue her. At the same time help her to make wise choices, but when you have the privilege of being consulted for advice, ask her what she thinks or what she would do before you jump in with your conclusions or solution.

Engage with your young daughter in something in which she is currently absorbed. Sit on the floor in her room and ask her the names of all her dolls. One-on-one attention from Dad, focused on something in which she is interested, tells her she matters.

One father approached me at an airport and told me how, after hearing a talk I had given on fathers, he had tried out that idea. He went into his seven-year-old's room and asked her to tell him about her dolls. She replied, 'Would you like to see my ponies?' then produced three scrapbooks of pony photographs. After what seemed like hours of sitting on the floor, during which the father was nearly dying of cramp, she finally got to the last pony photo. 'That was one thing,' he said, 'but three days later she invited me back into the room, got out the scrapbooks and expected me to remember all the names of the ponies!'

Apologise for words inappropriately spoken

Remember that we are the big people who have the experience, wisdom and hopefully the ability to step back and take responsibility for our actions even if we are stressed and overworked. Sometimes a negative spiral can develop if your daughter is acting badly and you respond to her mood. If you find yourself speaking harshly to your daughter, try to give yourself and her some space; when your emotions have cooled offer her an apology for your harsh words. By doing this you will give her a sense of dignity and open up a way forward, even if the issue has not been resolved.

If things have become stressed and angry between you, perhaps you could put aside the issue and build some one-on-one time together. Taking a step back from the situation and actively thinking about what you might do to just spend some time with her is sometimes a key to getting back on track.

Unlock your daughters emotions

There's a magic phrase that will unlock your daughter's emotions and give you an opportunity to protect her. Even when she's just beginning to talk, start lots of questions with it: 'How did it make you feel when . . .'

Listen carefully to what she says, occasionally commenting with 'I understand' and 'That must really make you sad.'

Conversation is absolutely foundational in your relationship with your daughter — but it won't happen automatically.

It is a wise father that knows his own child.
— **William Shakespeare,** The Merchant of Venice

Be a playful parent

So you are the parent of a girl. Here is your chance to play again. Parenting doesn't always have to be a serious business; in fact, it is the 'feeling' of your home that your child will remember. Without your using sarcasm or put-downs, your daughter will learn to read the twinkle in your eye and the body language as you laugh and play with her. I often tell the story of my daughter asking me, 'Hey Dad, how many leaves on that tree?' I used to reply, '64,862 .... Oh, one fell off — that means there are only 64,861!' Yes, it was tongue in cheek, and yes, she knew I hadn't really counted, but it was our 'conspiracy' and my chance to play the hero.

hot tip ✪

- ✪ Get down on the floor and play with her. Establish 'Daddy time', after she has eaten her dinner or when you first arrive home. Greet your wife, then play a game. It can be the same one each night, but it is still fulfilling her need for your attention. When the playing is over you can then set boundaries and say, 'Now it is Daddy's time to talk to Mummy.'
- ✪ Laugh with your daughter. Be silly sometimes. Find things you can do together that are fun — like reading funny books and watching silly movies. Do unpredictable and crazy things. An occasional hysterical shriek is a great sound in any home! However, be careful about the kind of laughter you employ. 'I was just kidding' rarely fixes a clumsy attempt at person-directed humour. If it's at your daughter's expense, you'll pay.

Fire her dreams for the future

A dad can set his daughter's heart on fire with dreams of the future. I can see that our daughter Kim gets so much of her talent from her mother, but I'll claim the credit for giving her the guts and belief in herself to use those gifts.

I am still impressed by the way she chose her own route in life — as a youth worker, a corporate manager and an educator, her style is authentic.

She models all the best traits that women bring to the mix of what it is to be human. She values her friendships, has achieved success through honouring others' gifts as well as her own, and is currently delighting in parenting her boys and creatively supporting a husband completing postgraduate studies.

Keep your nerve

One dad who drove his daughter to school each morning found when she hit 14 it felt like he couldn't say anything without her reacting negatively. In his head he put it down to her age and tried to stay calm and unruffled by her reactions. Until finally, one day, as she was getting out of the car, she burst into tears and said, 'Oh Dad, we used to be such good friends . . . I don't know why we don't get on!'

Keep your nerve when your daughter is in her early teens, or she might decide that you are embarrassing and know nothing. Continue to be the big person, knowing that this is only a stage, and that you still have a role in setting boundaries and affirming her. Be assured that when this time of identity crises and oscillating emotions passes you will enjoy a lasting friendship with your confident, poised, loving and capable daughter.

hot tip ✪

- ✪ Character matters more than reputation. Be willing to apologise, be honest about mistakes and forgiving of your children's mistakes. Be prepared to move on.
- ✪ Make sacrifices when necessary. Take time off when your baby is born, to support her mother and bond with your daughter.
- ✪ Choose your battles – and stick to them. Always ask yourself, 'Is it really important?' If it is, then stick to your guns (unless she gives you a very good reason to give in).
- ✪ Plan regular dates and let your daughter decide what to do with the time. It might not be an expensive trip out – it might just be about allowing her to choose.

- Make your daughters feel important and smart. Have lots of age-appropriate questions for the littlies!

- Take her along with you whenever possible. Teach her how to greet adults. Arm her with the phrases 'Pleased to meet you', 'Thank you' and 'You're welcome!'

- On significant occasions – when she starts school, on her 16th birthday – write to your daughter. Pass on your wisdom about life and love.

in summary ✐

WHAT DAUGHTERS NEED FROM FATHERS

A daughter needs you to:

- Listen to her.
- Encourage her to take risks and seek challenges, to speak up and speak out, to ask questions and not always accept the answers given.
- Expect the best of her. Show her that you trust her, and she is likely to rise to your good expectations.
- Invest in the relationship; make sure there's time in your diary for her.
- Not take yourself too seriously.
- Be involved in your daughter's friendships; engage her friends in conversation.
- Stay calm!
- Laugh a lot. Be a kid again, sometimes. Dirt washes off, clothes dry out, hair colour fades, but memories stay for a long, long time.

Chapter 14

Growing girls with character and colour

My parents totally influenced me. Their mantra was always that . . . being beautiful from the inside out was what they valued . . . not in a cheesy way but in a cool way. I always got the feeling that they were stoked about me being their daughter and that they thought I was beautiful and clever. Because I knew that was what they valued, I looked out for that in others.

— **Jess,** *20*

I totally respected my parents, the way they lived by those values. They stuck up for things . . . They didn't just let things pass . . . They instilled that faith in you and you see how it affected their lives and how they treated other people.

— **Emma,** *20*

Inspiring girls

It is probably true to say that inside most girls is a feeling that they would love to be part of a great adventure. Many long to do something significant, to make their life count or to address a big social evil. We don't mean like the winners of beauty pageants, who say their goal is to end world hunger and all cruelty to animals, but a genuine sense of possibility about their life and their ability to contribute to and have an influence in the world.

Every girl wants to be beautiful, wise, capable and desired.

If you speak to eight- and 10-year-old girls, they are often very sure of themselves and confident about what they want to do with their lives. Unfortunately, as girls head towards adolescence they often lose themselves and look for approval from others, especially boys, and lose their dreams and sense of future. This is where we parents are so vital, in helping our girls to hold onto their dreams. They need to see their lives as full of promise, and you their parents must continue to affirm their ability to achieve those dreams.

Girls' achievements are more the result of their families' focus and expectations than of their innate intellectual capacity.

The girls who made the comments at the beginning of this chapter did not have easy or straightforward routes through adolescence. But the anchor that in the end made them choose their parents' values was that their parents had lived the way they wanted their children to live. When parents fail or lose their daughters' trust, girls will settle for shallow goals or false comforters.

In the early 1990s two sociologists and two investigative journalists surveyed 20,000 college-age young people, asking the question, 'What is the new American dream?' The results were published in a book called *The Day America Told the Truth*. The researchers expected to get answers like, 'I want to be the first woman president of the United States' or 'I want to be the doctor who discovers a cure for cancer or AIDs. In fact, none of the answers they had expected — idealistic answers such as these — rated higher than 4 per cent of the responses; 83 per cent of those questioned said they wanted to be rich, and 81 per cent wanted to be thin. The researchers commented that here was the best-nourished, best-educated and best-clothed generation ever and all they wanted to be was rich or skinny. They called it 'The day America lost its soul'.

What hadn't the parents of these young people done to lift their children's sights higher?

If we adopt mere beauty or wealth as our own values, it will be hard to ask for more from our daughters. While the goal of being a mother is a worthy one, and one we do not want to diminish for every woman who wishes to and is able to raise children, the happiest mothers tend to be those who are confident in their own abilities and training, who know how to nurture themselves as well as their children. Encourage your daughter's exposure to careers that she will find satisfying and will suit her talents, take her to work with you and inspire her with the possibilities of life. She is far more likely to have a satisfying life if she engages on an educational track where she will meet interesting, motivated colleagues and possible future partners with similar interests. Hopefully, she will give herself permission to take the time to parent her own children, but there is likely to be a time when she wishes to return to a career or a cause, and if she is already confident in her identity and competence all those doors will be open to her.

Encourage leadership

There is little doubt that some children are natural leaders. They seem to be born with the sort of demeanour and attitude that inspires confidence in others. You may not have a teenage daughter who has a contagious way of involving her friends, or one who is highly competitive and captain of her team or class. However, all young people can be leaders in some way, and elements of leadership can definitely be taught. Even natural leaders need parents to coach them in humility, courage and care for the weakest.

Leadership takes many forms — it may be having the courage to run the gauntlet of the peer group and intervene when another pupil is being bullied, to have the ability perhaps to turn around a negative situation with diplomacy: 'Hey, come and have lunch with us; Joanne and I have a spare seat next to us.'

The way a girl is coached and supported will help her to develop the character that marks a real leader. Teenagers are very sensitive to the opinions of their peers, and for them leadership will be a delicate dance of 'normality' and 'fitting in', alongside setting the pace or tone when leadership is called for.

American studies of twins have suggested that many of the qualities associated with leadership, such as authoritarianism, are inherited from parents. In his book *The Optimistic Child* Martin Seligman says that between a quarter and a half of a person's main personality traits are inherited from their parents. This suggests that between half and three-quarters of these traits are not inherited, but are acquired and learned throughout life and honed in real-life situations.

Leadership is not necessarily about waving a sword, charging the enemy, and hoping the cavalry will follow. It can mean a quiet conversation with a friend in the hope of guiding them to the answer to a problem. It can mean showing initiative, whether the situation is a car accident, launching a boat, being the last to escape danger after helping others, or calming an angry neighbour.

It is also about resilience. During hard times or in difficult situations, resilient people emerge with stronger characters, but it is the mentors in their lives who help them interpret these hard times and learn from them. As a parent you might tell your daughter: 'I am truly proud of the way you acted when the chips were down . . .'; 'The way you led that team was outstanding — you made everyone feel that they mattered, and they gave their best.'

Leadership is being able to inspire others to dig deeper and to make altruistic decisions. It affirms others and brings out the best in them. Women tend to lead more by using their strengths with relationships and cooperation, organising and networking, and using group decisions. Enjoy watching this side of your daughter's nature emerge. The truth is, most people are at some time privileged to influence others to follow in some way. We need to support our teenagers when they have the opportunity to practise leadership even in small ways.

Expect the best of your daughter and give her a high level of support. Get to know her strengths, natural talents and abilities, and have a vision of the 18-year-old you would like to see her become — one with poise, integrity, warmth and assurance in her own capabilities.

Look for positive role models and peer groups

Peer groups with fun, enthusiastic and 'go-for-it' lifestyles show your daughter a life of promise. Female role models like grandmothers, aunts and friends can share wisdom.

Expose your daughter to inspiring people who are making a difference. Mary remembers as a 16-year-old, in her final year at high school, going with the rest of her form to hear Gladys Aylward, otherwise known as 'The Small Woman', speak publicly.

Gladys, who was famous for her epic journey over the Himalayas in which she led a hundred Chinese orphans to safety, was a short, gritty and inspirational figure. Later a movie was made about her life, called *The Inn of the Sixth Happiness*, starring Ingrid Bergman. Mary tells how impressed she was by this single woman who had provided a home for abandoned children, and saved their lives by embarking on that remarkable journey through the mountains. As an idealistic teenager, she says, she was inspired by the strength of character of 'The Small Woman', and hoped that were she ever in a similar situation she would show the same grit and character. 'I hoped I would do the right thing and fight for the defenceless even in the face of incredible odds.' Thinking back on that occasion, Mary says it stands out for her as a moment when she heard someone who described herself as 'ordinary and poor' show remarkable leadership. She inspired those teenage girls to have aspirations about their own ability to lead with faith and courage.

Help your daughter to build a life with meaning

Dr Jillian Arago, principal of Chilton St James School for Girls in Lower Hutt, suggests that we often allow our girls to quit before they have followed through on a commitment to an activity or sport. As soon as a certain amount of effort or 'stickability' is required, we allow them to opt out. In allowing them to become 'serial activity junkies', as she describes them, we rob them of the experience and importance of 'struggle' — and 'that's the thing that matters', she says.

Encourage your daughter to become involved in things that challenge, grow and extend her. Let her enjoy opportunities for wonderful, safe fun. Support positive friendships and get to know the parents of her friends, surrounding her with the community that is vital to a girl's identity. Encourage a variety of friendship groups. Learn what she learns — get involved and discuss her opinions. Expose your daughter to inspirational female role models and heroines, letting her know that she can build a balanced life with meaning.

When speaking to teenagers, we often use the principles from the Parents Inc. *Attitude* programme for schools. Everyone can build a life of meaning by understanding that more than one area of life makes up who we become: we all need a self to live with; a work to live for; a faith to live by, and a great cause worthy of our lives. Make sure your daughter has something that will engage her imagination and draw her into a world of meaning. She should realise that girls can do anything, but that she needn't fall into the trap of believing she has to do everything, especially at the same time. It is important for girls to learn from successful women that the journey they have taken is usually a series of episodes.

Give her 'her voice'; champion her self-reliance

Educating girls requires a different approach from that which is appropriate for boys. Girls go through a different journey in their education. Their brains are different; they have a different hormone set. Oestrogen and progesterone act on a girl's amygdala, the seat of the emotions, as a 'downer'. This has a very powerful effect on them and makes them retreat into themselves.

Consequently the need for 'encouragement', which we have emphasised throughout this book, is not a sentimental indulgence but life-giving for girls. Dr Arago says this is important because 'good self-esteem is not the hallmark of the adolescent girl'. As she says, 'You can praise a girl a hundred times and then make one remark that could be construed as negative, and that is the one she will remember.'

We need to allow our girls to be ambitious, and to empower their imagination, encouraging them to give themselves permission to succeed. However, they will learn from other women that most people's lives are made up of swings and roundabouts. They will need skills and abilities, but they also need to know how to be innovative and adaptable, and how to bounce back from disappointments.

Dr Sylvia Rimm and her daughter Sara researched and documented the lives of thousands of successful women in the US. They defined success as 'personal fulfilment', and reported their findings in the book *How Jane Won*. The interesting thing was that they found this category of success among a huge range of women. While differing in personality and ability, ethnicity and background, there was a resourcefulness among these women that allowed them to make choices that were right for them, and to achieve a balance and 'sequencing' in what they did. Many had sequenced their lives by putting a higher priority on either relationships or work at different stages of their lives.

Sylvia Rimm suggests that parents always make sure their daughter knows their recommendations are based on their love and wanting the best for her. She also suggests that parents communicate that for most girls and women balancing work and relationships will be an on-going challenge throughout their lives, and that it is okay to make decisions that fulfil your own values, not be squashed into societal expectations.

GUIDELINES FOR GIRLS

In How Jane Won *Sylvia Rimm translated her conclusions about successful women into guidelines for girls. Here are some of those guidelines in summary:*

Girls grow through healthy competition
Encourage your daughter to take the risk of entering competitions in either her school or work world. She should be encouraged to enter both competitions where she feels confident so she can experience the exhilaration of winning, but also enter some in which she feels less skilled. Admiring, praising or learning from those who are doing better than her gives a sense of personal control, and competitors are more likely to give her a boost when she needs it. There will always be those who do better than her and those who do less well.

Girls who see themselves as smart are poised to succeed

Feeling smart doesn't mean that a girl has to feel capable in every area. Finding her strengths and interests will help her feel good about herself.

Being social is neither good nor bad but it shouldn't interfere with learning

Being social is fine as long as her social life doesn't interfere with learning during her crucial school years. Encourage her to choose friends who share the values that matter most to you as a family. If she has friends who value learning, they're likely to support each other and still find time for fun.

Successful women see travel as a major positive experience

They often describe travel with their families as adventurous or as an opportunity for family bonding. Travel with school groups during high school and college had dramatic effects on their independence and broadened their perspectives.

Siblings needn't hold you back

Just because she is not the eldest don't let that stop her from taking on leadership roles or, if she is the eldest, from stepping back and letting others take the lead.

Opportunities spring from obstacles

Prepare to be challenged and get support to meet obstacles. Her pathway to success is likely to be indirect. A balance of control and creativity is important for most careers. Successful women have a passion for their work.

Balance passion with reason

Consider the values to be derived from a career. Encourage her to not commit herself to one career direction too early or stay in one when she knows she has hit a wall.

Raising a strong daughter

Give your daughter the resources and confidence to face the world and care for herself. Encourage her strength and celebrate her savvy. Help her learn to recognise, resist and overcome barriers. Help her develop her strengths to achieve her goals, help other people and help herself. Help her be what the American organisation Girls Incorporated calls 'strong, smart and bold'!

Remember that the investment you make while your daughter is in your home will be an investment in your future. As you coach her in wisdom and competence, your daughter is likely to grow into a loving adult who will become a close friend and confidante, bringing you great joy in the way she operates as an adult and raises her own children. The real pay-off for you, however, as I often say, will be that a confident and strong daughter will fight for the sunny room in the retirement home for you as her parent!

Finally, when we conclude an evening of speaking to parents about girls I usually finish with a poem that was for many years on Mother Teresa's office wall in Calcutta. It is often credited to Mother Teresa herself, but was actually written by a student leader in the 1970s when so much that was traditional was being rebelled against by students. Protest, a culture of dropping out, self-analysis and anger were hallmarks of the era. Keith Kent wrote this poem, offering students a way of contributing and standing tall without buying into the materialism and power structures that were such anathema to them.

We wish you fun, love and an exhilarating journey in parenting your daughter.

Anyway

People are often unreasonable, illogical and self-centred;
Forgive them anyway.

If you are kind, people may accuse you of selfish, ulterior motives;
Be kind anyway.

If you are successful, you will win some false friends and some genuine enemies;
Succeed anyway.

If you are honest and sincere, people may deceive you;
Be honest and sincere anyway.

What you spend years building, someone could destroy overnight;
Build anyway.

If you find serenity and happiness, some may be jealous;
Be happy anyway.

The good you do today, will often be forgotten tomorrow;
Do good anyway.

Give the world the best you have, and it may never be enough;
Give the world your best anyway.

You see, in the final analysis, it is between you and God;
It was never between you and them anyway.

Dr Kent Keith (located on Mother Teresa's wall in Calcutta)

Bibliography and suggested reading

Biddulph, Steve, *Raising Babies*, London, HarperCollins, 2006.

Brizendine, Louann, *The Female Brain*, New York, Morgan Road Books, 2006.

Campbell, Ross, *How to Really Love Your Child*, Colorado Springs, CO, David C. Cook, 2004.

Carr-Gregg, Michael, *The Princess Bitchface Syndrome: Surviving Adolescent Girls*, Melbourne, Penguin, 2006.

Chapman, Gary, *The Five Love Languages of Teenagers*, Chicago, Northfield Publishing, 2000.

Chapman, Gary, and Campbell, Ross, *The Five Love Languages of Children*, Chicago, Northfield Publishing, 1997.

Cline, Foster, and Clay, Jim, *Parenting Teens with Love and Logic*, Pinon Press, 2006.

Cohen, Lawrence J., *Playful Parenting*, New York, Ballantine, 2001.

Coloroso, Barbara, *Kids Are Worth It!* Port Melbourne, Lothian, 1995.

—— *The Bully, the Bullied and the Bystander: From Preschool to High School – How Parents and Teachers Can Help Break the Cycle of Violence*, New York, HarperCollins, 2003.

Cowan, John, Grant, Mary and Heilman, Craig, *Sex with Attitude*, Auckland, Parenting with Confidence, 1996.

Deak, JoAnn, with Teresa Barker, *Girls Will Be Girls: Raising Confident and Courageous Daughters*, New York, Hyperion, 2002.

Dellasega, Sheryl and Nixon, Charisse, *Girl Wars: 12 Strategies That Will End Female Bullying*, New York, Simon & Schuster, 2003.

DeVillers, Julia, *GirlWise: How to Be Confident, Capable, Cool, and in Control*, New York, Three Rivers Press, 2002.

Eldredge, John, *Wild at Heart: Discovering the Secret of a Man's Soul*, Nashville, Nelson Books, 2001.

Eldredge, John and Eldredge, Stasi, *Captivating: Unveiling the Mystery of a Woman's Soul*, Nashville, Thomas Nelson, 2005.

Godfrey, Neale S., *A Penny Saved*, New York, Fireside Books/Simon & Schuster, 1995.

Godfrey, Neale S., Edwards, Carolina, and Richards, Tad, *Money Doesn't Grow on Trees: A Parent's Guide to Raising Financially Responsible Children*, New York, Fireside Books, 1994.

Grant, Mary, *Cappuccino Moments for Mothers*, Auckland, Lime Grove House, 2000.

Gurian, Michael, *The Wonder of Girls: Understanding the Hidden Nature of Our Daughters*, New York, Atria Books, 2002.

—— *Boys and Girls Learn Differently! A Guide for Teachers and Parents*, San Francisco, Jossey-Bass, 2001.

Kerr, Barbara, *Smart Girls: A New Psychology of Girls, Women, and Giftedness*, Scottsdale, AZ, Great Potential Press, 1994.

King, Laughton, *With, Not Against*, Self published, 2006.

Lamb, Sharon, *The Secret Lives of Girls*, New York, The Free Press, 2001.

Littauer, Florence, *Personality Plus: How To Understand Others by Understanding Yourself*, Grand Rapids, Fleming H. Revel/Baker Publishing Group, 1992.

Mackoff, Barbara, *Growing a Girl: Seven Strategies for Raising a Strong, Spirited Daughter*, New York, Dell, 1996.

Malcolm, Jo, *Kiwi Dads: A Celebration of New Zealand Heroes*, Auckland, Hodder Moa Beckett, 2003.

McGraw, Phil, *Family First*, New York, Free Press, 2005.

McMillan, Karen, *Feast or Famine: A New Zealand Guide to Understanding Eating Disorders*, Auckland, Random House, 2006.

Miller, Donald, *Searching for God Knows What*, Nashville, Thomas Nelson, 2004.

Moir, Anne and Jessel, David, *Brain Sex: The Real Difference Between Men and Women*, New York, Dell, 1989.

Nelsen, Jane, *Positive Discipline*, New York, Ballantyne Books, 1981.

Nerburn, Kent, *Simple Truths: Clear and Gentle Guidance on the Big Issues of Life*, Navato, CA, New World Library, 1996.

Orenstein, Peggy, *Schoolgirls: Young Women, Self Esteem, and the Confidence Gap*, New York, Anchor Books, 1995, 2000.

Palmer, Sue, *Detoxing Childhood*, London, Orion, 2006.

Patterson, James and Kim, Peter, *The Day America Told the Truth*, New York, Prentice Hall, 1991.

Pipher, Mary, *Reviving Ophelia: Saving the Selves of Adolescent Girls*, New York, Putnam, 1994.

Preuschoff, Gisela, *Raising Girls*, London, Harper Thorsons, 2005.

Rimm, Sylvia, *See Jane Win: A Smart Girl's Guide to Success*, Minneapolis, Free Spirit Publishing, 2003.

—— *How Jane Won: 55 Successful Women Share How They Grew from Ordinary Girls to Extraordinary Women*, New York, Three Rivers Press, 2001.

Sax, Leonard, *Why Gender Matters: What Parents and Teachers Need to Know About the Emerging Science of Sex Differences*, New York, Doubleday, 2005.

Schlessinger, Laura, *How Could You Do That?! The Abdication of Character, Courage, and Conscience*, New York, HarperCollins, 1997.

Schlessinger, Laura, and Vogel, Stewart, *The Ten Commandments: The Significance of God's Laws in Everyday Life*, New York, HarperCollins, 1998.

Seligman, Martin E.P., *The Optimistic Child: A Proven Program to Safeguard Children from Depression and Build Lifelong Resilience*, Boston, Houghton Mifflin, 1995.

Thompson, Peter, *Wisdom: The Hard-Won Gift*, Sydney, ABC Books, 2001.

Trent, John, and Smalley, Gary, *The Treasure Tree: Helping Kids Understand Their Personality*, Nashville, Tommy Nelson, 1992.

Vitz, Paul, *Faith of the Fatherless: The Psychology of Atheism*, Dallas, Spence Publishing, 2000.

Weaver, Stephanie, *Teenage Girls Talk: 52 New Zealand Teenagers Talk about Their Lives*, Auckland, Random House, 2002.

CDs

The Big Weekend, available from www.parentsinc.org.nz

Useful websites

www.parentsinc.org.nz
www.genderdifferences.org/hearing.htm
www.theparentingplace.com

Index

GROWING
GREAT BOYS

100s
of **practical**
strategies for
bringing out
the **best** in
your
son

Ian
Grant

communicate

ian grant

how to speak well
in public and in private!